T0194685

An Analysis of

Sigmund Freud's

The Interpretation of Dreams

William J. Jenkins

Published by Macat International Ltd
24:13 Coda Centre, 189 Munster Road, London SW6 6AW.

Distributed exclusively by Routledge
2 Park Square, Milton Park, Abingdon, Oxon OX14 4RN
711 Third Avenue, New York, NY 10017, USA

Routledge is an imprint of the Taylor & Francis Group, an informa business

www.macat.com
info@macat.com

Cataloguing in Publication Data
A catalogue record for this book is available from the British Library.
Library of Congress Cataloguing-in-Publication Data is available upon request.
Cover illustration: Etienne Gilfillan

ISBN 978-1-912303-56-4 (hardback)
ISBN 978-1-912127-43-6 (paperback)
ISBN 978-1-912282-44-9 (e-book)

Notice
The information in this book is designed to orientate readers of the work under analysis,
to elucidate and contextualise its key ideas and themes, and to aid in the development
of critical thinking skills. It is not meant to be used, nor should it be used, as a
substitute for original thinking or in place of original writing or research. References and
notes are provided for informational purposes and their presence does not constitute
endorsement of the information or opinions therein. This book is presented solely for
educational purposes. It is sold on the understanding that the publisher is not engaged
to provide any scholarly advice. The publisher has made every effort to ensure that
this book is accurate and up-to-date, but makes no warranties or representations with
regard to the completeness or reliability of the information it contains. The information
and the opinions provided herein are not guaranteed or warranted to produce particular
results and may not be suitable for students of every ability. The publisher shall not be
liable for any loss, damage or disruption arising from any errors or omissions, or from
the use of this book, including, but not limited to, special, incidental, consequential or
other damages caused, or alleged to have been caused, directly or indirectly, by the
information contained within.

CONTENTS

THE MACAT LIBRARY

The Macat Library is a series of unique academic explorations of seminal works in the humanities and social sciences – books and papers that have had a significant and widely recognised impact on their disciplines. It has been created to serve as much more than just a summary of what lies between the covers of a great book. It illuminates and explores the influences on, ideas of, and impact of that book. Our goal is to offer a learning resource that encourages critical thinking and fosters a better, deeper understanding of important ideas.

Each publication is divided into three Sections: Influences, Ideas, and Impact. Each Section has four Modules. These explore every important facet of the work, and the responses to it.

This Section-Module structure makes a Macat Library book easy to use, but it has another important feature. Because each Macat book is written to the same format, it is possible (and encouraged!) to cross-reference multiple Macat books along the same lines of inquiry or research. This allows the reader to open up interesting interdisciplinary pathways.

To further aid your reading, lists of glossary terms and people mentioned are included at the end of this book (these are indicated by an asterisk [*] throughout) – as well as a list of works cited.

Macat has worked with the University of Cambridge to identify the elements of critical thinking and understand the ways in which six different skills combine to enable effective thinking.
Three allow us to fully understand a problem; three more give us the tools to solve it. Together, these six skills make up the **PACIER** model of critical thinking. They are:

ANALYSIS – understanding how an argument is built
EVALUATION – exploring the strengths and weaknesses of an argument
INTERPRETATION – understanding issues of meaning

CREATIVE THINKING – coming up with new ideas and fresh connections
PROBLEM-SOLVING – producing strong solutions
REASONING – creating strong arguments

To find out more, visit **WWW.MACAT.COM.**

CRITICAL THINKING AND *THE INTERPRETATION OF DREAMS*

Primary critical thinking skill: INTERPRETATION
Secondary critical thinking skill: ANALYSIS

There is arguably no more famous book about the arts of interpretation and analysis than Sigmund Freud's 1899 *The Interpretation of Dreams*. Though the original edition of just 600 copies took eight years to sell out, the book eventually became a classic text that helped cement Freud's reputation as one of the most significant intellectual figures of the 19th and 20th centuries.

In critical thinking, just as in Freud's psychoanalytical theories, interpretation is all about understanding the meaning of evidence, and tracing the significance of things. Analysis can then be brought in to tease out the implicit reasons and assumptions that lie underneath the interpreted evidence.

The Interpretation of Dreams is a masterclass in building telling analyses from ingenious interpretation of evidence. Freud worked from the assumption that all dreams were significant attempts by the unconscious to resolve conflicts. As a result, he argued, they contain in altered and disguised forms clues to our deepest unconscious urges and desires. Each must be taken on its own terms to tease out what they really mean. Though Freud's theories have often been criticized, he remains the undisputed master of interpretation – with his critics suggesting that he was, if anything, too ingenious for his own good.

ABOUT THE AUTHOR OF THE ORIGINAL WORK

Sigmund Freud, "the father of psychoanalysis," was born in Vienna, Austria, in 1856. He studied medicine at the University of Vienna before opening a private practice in his hometown. His work with physician Josef Breuer on treating nervous disorders led to a book, *Studies on Hysteria*. Freud built on that—as well as on his work with private patients and analysis of his own dreams—to formulate the psychological theories he laid out in *The Interpretation of Dreams*. The text made him a celebrity, but it also revolutionized the treatment of mental illness. Just before Nazi Germany annexed Austria in 1938, Freud (who was Jewish) fled to England with his family. He died in London the following year at the age of 83.

ABOUT THE AUTHOR OF THE ANALYSIS

Dr Bill Jenkins holds a PhD in psychology from the University of Michigan. He is currently co-chair of the Department of Psychology at Mercer University in Georgia.

ABOUT MACAT

GREAT WORKS FOR CRITICAL THINKING

Macat is focused on making the ideas of the world's great thinkers accessible and comprehensible to everybody, everywhere, in ways that promote the development of enhanced critical thinking skills.

It works with leading academics from the world's top universities to produce new analyses that focus on the ideas and the impact of the most influential works ever written across a wide variety of academic disciplines. Each of the works that sit at the heart of its growing library is an enduring example of great thinking. But by setting them in context – and looking at the influences that shaped their authors, as well as the responses they provoked – Macat encourages readers to look at these classics and game-changers with fresh eyes. Readers learn to think, engage and challenge their ideas, rather than simply accepting them.

'Macat offers an amazing first-of-its-kind tool for interdisciplinary learning and research. Its focus on works that transformed their disciplines and its rigorous approach, drawing on the world's leading experts and educational institutions, opens up a world-class education to anyone.'

Andreas Schleicher
Director for Education and Skills, Organisation for Economic Co-operation and Development

'Macat is taking on some of the major challenges in university education ... They have drawn together a strong team of active academics who are producing teaching materials that are novel in the breadth of their approach.'

Prof Lord Broers,
former Vice-Chancellor of the University of Cambridge

'The Macat vision is exceptionally exciting. It focuses upon new modes of learning which analyse and explain seminal texts which have profoundly influenced world thinking and so social and economic development. It promotes the kind of critical thinking which is essential for any society and economy. This is the learning of the future.'

Rt Hon Charles Clarke, former UK Secretary of State for Education

'The Macat analyses provide immediate access to the critical conversation surrounding the books that have shaped their respective discipline, which will make them an invaluable resource to all of those, students and teachers, working in the field.'

Professor William Tronzo, University of California at San Diego

WAYS IN TO THE TEXT

KEY POINTS

- Sigmund Freud was an Austrian neurologist* (a specialist in the nervous system and brain) and the founder of the therapeutic and theoretical approach to the unconscious mind* known as psychoanalysis.*

- In *The Interpretation of Dreams*, Freud argues that we can understand the wishes of the unconscious mind by analyzing and interpreting the meaning of dreams.

- Scholars consider *The Interpretation of Dreams* to be Freud's most important work; it has greatly influenced the fields of psychology* (the study of the human mind and behavior) and psychiatry* (the treatment of disorders of the mind).

Who Was Sigmund Freud?

Born in 1856, Sigmund Freud lived most of his life in Vienna, Austria. After receiving his medical degree from the University of Vienna in 1881, he worked in the psychiatric unit at a local hospital. This gave him hands-on experience of working with individuals who suffered from mental illnesses.

In 1885, Freud studied under the famed French neurologist Jean-Martin Charcot.* While working with Charcot, Freud realized that many psychological disorders trace back to traumatic events earlier in a patient's life. These events get stored in the unconscious mind. In 1893, the Austrian physician Josef Breuer* told Freud about his work with a patient who had some unusual physical symptoms with no obvious physical causes. Rather than treat the patient medically, Breuer began to engage in a form of therapy in which the patient talked about his experiences. Over time, Breuer found that this "talking cure" improved his patient's symptoms. In 1895, Freud and Breuer described this new therapeutic approach in a book called *Studies on Hysteria*.

Freud's experiences with Charcot and Breuer inspired his ideas about the role the unconscious mind plays in determining behavior. He began to view dreams as one way the unconscious mind communicates its desires. Freud's 1899 masterwork *The Interpretation of Dreams* became wildly popular and helped establish the psychoanalytic perspective in psychology and psychiatry. The work has since been published around the world and remains in print more than a century later.

What Does *The Interpretation of Dreams* Say?

Before Freud, most people believed that dreams had no purpose and no meaning. Freud made the radical argument that dreams, created by the unconscious mind, in fact contain a great deal of meaning.

In *The Interpretation of Dreams*, Freud argues that dreams contain meaningful information about the dreamer's unfulfilled, unconscious wishes. Each dream, he claims, is a message in disguise; one must interpret its meaning through dream analysis:* the process of talking through the associations the dreamer might hold for what the dream contains.

Freud begins *The Interpretation of Dreams* by reviewing the existing literature on dreams. He discusses the ancient idea that dreams were the work of spirits or demons. He also examines the more contemporary notion that dreams represent extensions of the waking state or neural activity* (electrical and chemical processes at the level of cells) in the brain's sensory regions.

Freud demonstrates how to analyze and interpret a dream. He describes engaging the patient in free association* as he considers each aspect of the dream. In free association, one person (the therapist, for instance) says a word and the other (the patient) responds immediately with another word. The words may have no any obvious connection, but the therapist can use the sequence to interpret the workings of the patient's unconscious mind.

Freud also showed that all dreams represent the fulfillment of some unconscious wish. Our conscious minds censor these wishes in some way, so they manifest in our dreams. The dream story, or "manifest content,"* hides the dream's true meaning, or "latent" content.* Freud describes several ways in which the mind transforms wishes into dreams. This allows the reader to better engage in dream analysis.

The unconscious transforms wishes into dreams if they would be too uncomfortable to acknowledge in an uncensored form. According to Freud, many of these wishes represent sexual impulses. These sexual impulses often get established early in life, as a child interacts with his or her parents. Freud believed that it was a normal part of human development for children to direct sexual and aggressive impulses at their parents. In his view, the difference between healthy people and those suffering from psychological problems is that the latter group exaggerated these normal impulses.

Freud describes his rough theory of mind* in terms of reflex circuits*—simple connections in which the mind receives sensory information and the body responds by acting in some way. This biological conception of the mind, common in his day, reflected Freud's training and background as a physician. He saw the mind as consisting of two parts: unconscious and conscious. With no direct access to the conscious mind, the unconscious mind relies on dreams to convey its wants and desires into the realm of consciousness.* This idea served as a foundation for much of Freud's later work and distinguished him from many of his peers.

Why Does *The Interpretation of Dreams* Matter?

Scholars generally consider *The Interpretation of Dreams* to be Freud's most significant work. In it, he lays the foundation for many of his future ideas. It helped established the psychoanalytic school of thought in the fields of psychology and psychiatry. It also offers a technique for treating psychological problems. The psychoanalytic school emphasizes the role that the unconscious mind plays in motivating conscious behavior. Freud also developed a "stage theory" of psychosexual development,* which used principles of psychoanalysis to explain (very roughly) normal human development in terms of stages differing in the source of sexual pleasure. Freud believed that an adult's personality* traits reflect the resolution of sexual impulses as that person passed through the various stages of development.

The Interpretation of Dreams and Freud's psychoanalytic perspective played a great part in shaping the disciplines of both psychology and psychiatry. The work helped people think about the unconscious mind in entirely new ways (the idea that dreams carry meaningful information from the unconscious, for example). As Freud's ideas inspired followers, the psychoanalytic perspective grew more influential. Some of the people inspired by his work held different opinions of the exact nature of the unconscious mind and about the importance of sexual impulses. As a result of these disagreements, some followers established their own perspectives; with ideas clearly based on Freud's original conception, these people are called "neo-Freudians."*

The criticisms the text inspired may be as important as the text itself. Almost from the outset, some of Freud's contemporaries dismissed his ideas as flawed. Critics saw them as overly anecdotal (specific examples that cannot be considered truly representative), since they arose from the work Freud had done with his patients and from his own self-analysis. Beyond being anecdotal, they were not testable. Science demands that ideas be repeatable and verifiable—but no one can observe the unconscious mind. Although the work may have seemed unscientific, Freud clearly valued science; this becomes clear on reading the text. Still, advances in science may open the door to exploring old ideas in new ways, enabling us to better verify the conclusions Freud drew from his and his patients' experiences.

SECTION 1
INFLUENCES

THE AUTHOR AND THE HISTORICAL CONTEXT

KEY POINTS

- *The Interpretation of Dreams* lays the groundwork for Freud's theories, which went on to become very influential and changed psychology*—the study of the human mind and behavior—forever.

- Freud's analysis of his own dreams and the death of his father served as a springboard for *The Interpretation of Dreams*.

- The morality of the Victorian era*—the period bridging the nineteenth and early twentieth centuries marked by the reign of the British monarch Queen Victoria—dominated Europe during much of Freud's life, playing a large part in shaping his theories.

Why Read This Text?

The Interpretation of Dreams is Sigmund Freud's most famous work. Published in 1899, it cemented his reputation as the father of the theoretical and therapeutic model of the psychoanalytic* movement that dominated the field of psychology for several decades.[1] Although many of his original ideas have proven problematic, Freud has undoubtedly been one of the most influential figures in the history of psychology. Indeed, as one scholar noted, "Freud has been ranked along with [the political philosopher Karl] Marx,* [the foundational evolutionary theorist Charles] Darwin,* and [the physicist Albert] Einstein* as the several geniuses who have put their imprints so very decisively upon the ways in which we have to come understand the

> ❝ The dream proves to be the first link in a chain of abnormal psychic* structures whose other links, the hysterical phobia,* the obsession,* and the delusion* must, for practical reasons, claim the interest of the physician. ❞
>
> Sigmund Freud, *The Interpretation of Dreams*

world in which we live and our place in it."[2] So influential was Freud that "our very language was … saturated with 'Freudian' meaning, slips* of the tongue, repression,* projection,* rationalization,* defenses,* and so forth"—all terms taken from Freudian theory, relating to unconscious speech, the unconscious mind* and behavior, and the therapeutic process.[3]

The Austrian psychiatrist* A. A. Brill* produced the first English translation of the book in 1913. He called *The Interpretation of Dreams* "the author's greatest and most important work."[4] In the book, Freud established the foundation on which he built his theories of the human mind and personality.* The book also guided other professionals who followed in Freud's footsteps as psychoanalysts. It represents an important text in the history of psychoanalysis and psychology, offering the reader insight into Freud's ideas about the important role dreams play in conveying information about the unconscious mind.

Author's Life

Born in 1856, Sigmund Freud spent most of his life in his home city of Vienna, Austria. He studied medicine at the University of Vienna, receiving his medical degree in 1881. The following year, he became a clinical assistant at the Vienna General Hospital, where he worked in the psychiatric clinic under neuropathologist* Theodor Meynert* (neuropathology is the study of disorders of the nervous system and brain). In 1885, Freud received a scholarship to study with the Frenchman considered "the father of neurology,"* Jean-Martin Charcot.* Charcot taught Freud about the symptoms of hysteria* (a neurotic* disorder characterized by extreme emotion) and how to treat them using hypnosis.*[5]

Returning to Vienna, Freud opened a private practice specializing in treating patients with nervous disorders. In 1893, he began to collaborate with the Austrian physician Josef Breuer.* The two men cowrote the book *Studies on Hysteria*,[6] (1895) which introduced free association*—a method in which patients are asked to offer immediate responses to words given to them by the psychoanalyst—as a therapeutic technique to treat hysteria. During this period, Freud also began to analyze and interpret some of his own dreams. He documented the experience, along with his work with patients and the death of his father, in *The Interpretation of Dreams.* In his preface to the book's second edition, Freud described it as "a part of my self-analysis, a reaction to the death of my father—that is, to the most significant event, the deepest loss, in the life of a man."[7]

After the first edition of *The Interpretation of Dreams* was published in 1899, Freud established what came to be known as the Vienna Psychoanalytic Society. He published several more books over the course of his career, elaborating on the ideas introduced in *Interpretation*. As a secular Jew, Freud was affected by the anti-Semitic* sentiments emanating from nearby Nazi Germany* (anti-Semitism is hostility to Jewish people). Germany annexed Austria in 1938, and Freud and his family fled to England a few months later. He died in London on September 23, 1939.[8]

Author's Background
The Swiss psychiatrist Carl Jung,* who studied with Freud, said that "the historical conditions which preceded Freud and formed his groundwork made a phenomenon like himself necessary."[9] Indeed,

the times in which Freud lived played a large role in the formation of some of his ideas. One of the strongest of these influences was the Victorian morality so pronounced in late nineteenth-century Europe. Victorians exhibited an "intense moral preoccupation with sexuality … Sexuality not only needed to be regulated by personal morality, or by the vigilance of the family, but, since it could affect entire populations, was a political and social concern."[10]

During this period, society also became increasingly interested in "scientific materialism* [here the assumption that all mental processes are a function of the brain] and [the logically-oriented philosophical position of] rationalism,"* wrote Jung. "This is the matrix out of which Freud grew, and it is the mental characteristics of this matrix which have shaped him along foreordained lines."[11]

Freud believed that the unconscious mind influences our behavior. We can tap into the unfulfilled wishes of the unconscious by analyzing our dreams. Given the sexual repression of the Victorian era, we should not be surprised that Freud believed the unconscious mind played a central role in repressing sexual attitudes and urges.

NOTES

1   B. M. Thorne and T. B. Henley, *Connections in the History and Systems of Psychology* (Boston, MA: Houghton Mifflin Company, 2005).

2   Robert S. Wallerstein, "The Relevance of Freud's Psychoanalysis in the 21st Century: Its Science and Its Research," *Psychoanalytic Psychology* 23, no. 2 (2006): 302–26.

3   Wallerstein, "The Relevance of Freud's Psychoanalysis," 303.

4   Sigmund Freud, *The Interpretation of Dreams*, translated by A. A. Brill, with an introduction and notes by Daniel T. O'Hara and Gina Masucci MacKenzie (New York: Barnes & Noble Books, 2005), 9.

5   Freud, *The Interpretation of Dreams*, xi–xii.

6   Sigmund Freud and Josef Breuer, *Studies on Hysteria*, trans. James Strachey (London: Hogarth Press, 1955).

7   Freud, *The Interpretation of Dreams*, 6.

8   Freud, *The Interpretation of Dreams,* XIII–XIX.

9   C. G. Jung, "Sigmund Freud in His Historical Setting," *Journal of Personality* 1, no. 1 (1932), 48–55.

10 "Historical Context for the Writings of Sigmund Freud," *Columbia College: The Core Curriculum*, accessed January 2, 2016, http://www.college. columbia.edu/core/content/writings-sigmund-freud/context.

11 Jung, "Sigmund Freud in His Historical Setting," 49.

MODULE 2
ACADEMIC CONTEXT

KEY POINTS

- While many view Sigmund Freud as the father of the therapeutic methods and theories of psychoanalysis,* the foundation for the psychoanalytic perspective was actually laid by the German physician and hypnotist* Franz Anton Mesmer* some 80 years before Freud's birth.

- By the time Freud entered the field, neuropsychiatry*—the field examining the role of the nervous system in disorders of the mind—had taken a primarily biological perspective in explaining psychological disorders.

- Freud's work with both the physicians Jean-Martin Charcot* and Josef Breuer* greatly influenced him in establishing the perspective of psychoanalysis.

The Work in its Context

Many consider *The Interpretation of Dreams* to be Sigmund Freud's most important work. It established psychoanalysis (sometimes called psychodynamic* therapy—a school of thought that emphasizes the role of unconscious forces in shaping behavior) as a dominant perspective in the fields of psychology* and psychiatry.*

Freud asserted that the unconscious mind* profoundly influences our conscious behavior and personality.* This new perspective created fundamental shifts in the disciplines that treated psychological disorders. Indeed, they would go on to rock the culture as a whole. But Freud did not introduce the concept of the unconscious mind. Some have argued that "a clash between the physician [Franz Anton] Mesmer and the exorcist [Johann Joseph] Gassner"*[1] in 1775 laid the foundations for psychoanalysis and the concept of the unconscious

> ❝ With Freud begins the era of the newer dynamic schools, with their official doctrine, their rigid organization, their specialized journals, their closed membership, and the prolonged initiation imposed upon their members. ❞
>
> Henri F. Ellenberger, *The Discovery of the Unconscious: The History and Evolution of Dynamic Psychiatry*

mind. ("Exorcism" is the ritual expulsion of malign forces such as demons from the troubled body.)

Gassner, a very popular healer, used religious techniques to rid people of various maladies. By 1775, as the rationality of the intellectual and social movement known as the Enlightenment* became more prominent in Europe, Gassner and his mystical cures came under suspicion. Mesmer provided an alternate perspective. Being a trained physician, he took a more scientific approach to the treatment of nervous disorders. Ultimately, the medical establishment rejected Mesmer's ideas. However, his opposition to spiritual modes of healing set a change into motion, and ultimately, clinical professionals adopted the psychoanalytic approach.[2]

Overview of the Field

The treatment of mental illness had already changed quite a bit by the time Sigmund Freud entered the profession. In the early days, people believed that mentally ill people were possessed by demons, so exorcists like Gassner treated them by spiritual means. By the late nineteenth century, most professionals in the field took a much more biological and systematic approach to understanding these disorders. They focused on tangible (that is, concrete), directly observed aspects of the person, such as their physical state. The shift toward science had been so complete that Freud felt compelled to write that his focus on the unconscious through dream analysis* had not "overstepped the bounds of neuropathological* interest"[3] ("neuropathology" here indicating disorders of the nervous system and brain). Referencing phobias* (irrational fears) and delusion* (false beliefs), he added, "one that cannot explain the origin of the dream pictures will strive in vain to understand the phobias, obsessive* and delusional ideas, and likewise their therapeutic importance."[4] Clearly, Freud worried that the establishment had largely discounted the influence of psychological factors on behavior.

However, some in the field shared Freud's views. They believed that both the unconscious mind and psychological factors influenced their patients' symptoms. Freud's work with these like-minded individuals, such as Charcot, in the formative years of his career helped him shape the ideas in *The Interpretation of Dreams.*

Academic Influences

A scholarship allowed Freud to study in Paris with the French physician Jean-Martin Charcot, whom many consider to be the father of neurology.* Charcot specialized in treating people with unusual symptoms that had no apparent physical cause. Over the course of his career, Charcot came to believe that his patients were experiencing "a form of hysteria* which had been induced by their emotional reaction to a traumatic accident in their past."[5] During his time with Charcot, Freud concluded that neuroses*—mental illnesses involving anxiety— originating from the unconscious mind caused these unusual symptoms.

Freud's collaborations with the respected Austrian physician Josef Breuer also deeply influenced him. Breuer helped Freud establish his own medical practice and in many ways served as one of his mentors. Breuer told Freud about one of his most interesting patients, a woman who came to be known as Anna O.* They would recount her story in the book they coauthored in 1895 entitled *Studies on Hysteria.*[6] Anna's bizarre symptoms included unexplained coughing, paralysis of one side of her body, and even vivid hallucinations. Ultimately, Breuer diagnosed her with hysteria. But he found that when he discussed the hallucinations with Anna, her symptoms faded. This talking cure intrigued Freud. Combining the ideas of trauma-induced hysteria with Breuer's form of therapy, Freud developed his unique approach. After Freud, free association* (the process in which a patient immediately responds to words, without self-censorship) and dream analysis (the process of discovering what the unconscious mind is communicating in dreams) would become cornerstones of psychoanalysis.[7]

NOTES

1   Henri F. Ellenberger, *The Discovery of the Unconscious: The History and Evolution of Dynamic Psychiatry* (New York: Basic Books, 2008), 53.

2   Ellenberger, *The Discovery of the Unconscious*, 53–7.

3   Sigmund Freud, *The Interpretation of Dreams*, translated by A. A. Brill, with an introduction and notes by Daniel T. O'Hara and Gina Masucci MacKenzie (New York: Barnes & Noble Books, 2005), 3.

4   Freud, *The Interpretation of Dreams*, 3.

5   Richard Webster, "Freud, Charcot, and Hysteria: Lost in the Labyrinth," accessed January 3, 2016, http://www.richardwebster.net/freudandcharcot.html.

6   Sigmund Freud and Josef Breuer, *Studies on Hysteria*, trans. James Strachey (London: Hogarth, 1955).

7   Webster, "Freud, Charcot, and Hysteria: Lost in the Labyrinth."

MODULE 3
THE PROBLEM

KEY POINTS

- Freud and his contemporaries wanted to better understand the psychological* causes of some mental illness.

- Most of Freud's colleagues sought physiological explanations for these disturbances. In doing so, they largely ignored the unconscious mind* and dream analysis.*

- Freud believed that the unconscious mind played an important role in causing many mental illnesses. He also held that dreams enabled the unconscious mind to reveal unfulfilled wishes.

Core Question

In *The Interpretation of Dreams*, Sigmund Freud presented his belief that dreams provide insight into the unconscious mind, and that analyzing them could help treat mental illness. At the time Freud wrote the book, the medical establishment paid little attention to dreams or the unconscious mind. They focused instead on trying to determine the physical causes of mental illnesses. Back then there were few technological resources to map out the nervous system. Instead, professionals proposed that behavior was a reflex circuit:* circuits, constructed in the brain, that involved sensory input* (things such as sight and hearing) and motor output* (physical action). Freud noted that "the reflex arc* remains the model for every psychic* activity"[1] so the theory of mind* he presented in *The Interpretation of Dreams* followed this essential organization.

> **❝ It is hard to deny the extent to which Freud's
> energetic theory of reflex diverged from the dominant
> nineteenth century conceptions. ❞**
> Nima Bassiri, "Freud and the Matter of the Brain"

In Freud's view, the core question of the day involved determining what role, if any, the unconscious mind plays in affecting conscious behavior. Assuming his emphasis on the unconscious was correct, in *The Interpretation of Dreams* Freud outlined a procedure other clinicians could use to analyze and interpret dreams. By couching these ideas in scientific language, Freud hoped that the book would appeal to a broad range of colleagues across the scientific and spiritual communities.

The Participants

Freud was convinced that some types of psychological disturbances were psychic rather than physical in nature. His work with both the French neurologist* Jean-Martin Charcot* and the Austrian physician Josef Breuer* only strengthened this belief, but many of his contemporaries disagreed. Freud had trained in medicine and developed his theories of psychoanalysis* from an increased commitment to a scientific understanding of the mind. But "Freud openly broke with official medicine"[2] by taking the position that mental illness could cause physical symptoms. Some critics considered the dream to be a simple "reaction to the stimulus causing a disturbance of sleep."[3] As such, the established medical position held that dreams served no real purpose. Without a purpose, they could offer no special understanding of either the human mind or the symptoms of hysteria.*

But Freud believed "the dream has a meaning, albeit a hidden one; that it is intended as a substitute for some other thought process, and that it is only a question of revealing this substitute correctly in order to reach the hidden signification of the dream."[4] He used *The Interpretation of Dreams* to communicate his ideas with his colleagues. Ultimately, he believed science would turn to his approach in treating individuals suffering from physical symptoms when doctors could identify no somatic—that is, body-based—abnormalities.

The Contemporary Debate

The idea of behavior as a reflex had become quite popular by the time Freud wrote *The Interpretation of Dreams.* Indeed, Freud himself had described behavior in terms of a reflex before he wrote the book. As one writer noted, "Freud defined reflex action as a tendency towards a state of inertia."*[5] Freud used "inertia" in a specific sense; it indicated "the tendency of the nervous system—and thus the psyche* [the mind] to discharge excessive buildups of excitation."[6] Freud and his contemporaries believed that people derived pleasure from this discharge of excess excitation. If this excitation was allowed to accumulate, however, it led to aversion—a desire to avoid something.

While Freud used the popular model of the time to introduce his ideas, his concept of reflex actually differed significantly from the more prominent, generally accepted ideas. Specifically, Freud's focus on the role of the unconscious mind bore little similarity to the connections between sensory and motor systems generally described as "reflexes." Critics noted the differences and attacked Freud's ideas about the mind and how dreams help us understand its operations. Despite the criticism, Freud sometimes felt ignored and unappreciated by the larger psychiatric* community. Indeed, in the preface to the second edition of his book, he remarked that, "the behavior of the scientific critics could only justify the expectation that this work of mine was destined to be buried in oblivion."[7]

NOTES

1   Sigmund Freud, *The Interpretation of Dreams*, translated by A. A. Brill, with an introduction and notes by Daniel T. O'Hara and Gina Masucci MacKenzie (New York: Barnes & Noble Books, 2005), 425.

2   Henri F. Ellenberger, *The Discovery of the Unconscious: The History and Evolution of Dynamic Psychiatry* (New York: Basic Books, 2008), 418.

3   Sigmund Freud, *The Interpretation of Dreams*, 73.

4   Freud, *The Interpretation of Dreams*, 89.

5   Nima Bassiri, "Freud and the Matter of the Brain: On the Rearrangements of Neuropsychoanalysis," *Critical Inquiry* 40, no. 1 (2013): 83–108.

6   Bassiri, "Freud and the Matter of the Brain," 91.

7   Freud, *The Interpretation of Dreams*, 5.

THE AUTHOR'S CONTRIBUTION

KEY POINTS

- Freud believed that the psyche,* or the mind, actively constructed dreams to communicate information about the dreamer's unfulfilled wishes or desires.

- Freud's focus on the unconscious mind* offered innovative, alternative explanations to the physical causes of psychological disorders.

- In *The Interpretation of Dreams*, Freud creatively synthesizes and extends the work he did with both the physicians Jean-Martin Charcot* and Josef Breuer.*

Author's Aims

In writing *The Interpretation of Dreams*, Sigmund Freud primarily wanted to convince the reader that dreams had significant meaning and that interpreting them would offer insight into the wishes and desires of the unconscious mind. These insights could then be used to treat mental illnesses. Freud spends the entire first chapter of the book discussing the current state of knowledge regarding dreams. He concludes, "notwithstanding the effort of several thousand years, little progress [had] been made in the scientific understanding of dreams."[1]

Nevertheless, he begins with an overview of various theories of dreams from the past. He mentions some of these ideas only in passing—such as the ancient belief that dreams resulted from the work of spirits. He sorted the more modern ideas into several broad categories:

- Theories that related dreams to the waking state
- Theories about dreams and memory

> ❝ In the following pages, I shall prove that there exists a psychological technique by which dreams may be interpreted, and that upon the application of this method every dream will show itself to be a senseful psychological structure which may be introduced into an assignable place in the psychic activity of the waking state. ❞
>
> Sigmund Freud, *The Interpretation of Dreams*

- Theories about dreams as disturbances of sleep or as reactions to stimuli
- Theories explaining why we forget dreams so easily on awaking
- Theories about differences in function of the mind between the dreaming and waking states
- The moral content of dreams
- Theories about the functions dreams might serve
- The relationship between mental illness and dreams.[2]

Devoting the balance of the text to reinforcing the importance of dreams and the insights they give us into the mind, Freud walks the reader through a sample dream and its interpretation. He notes that he learned from working with his patients "that a dream may be linked into the psychic* concatenation [sequence] which must be followed backwards into the memory from the pathological* idea as a starting point. The next step was to treat the dream as a symptom, and to apply to it the method of interpretation which had been worked out for such symptoms."[3]

Approach
The principles of the intellectual and social current known as the Enlightenment* that had been sweeping Europe since the seventeenth

century emphasized the importance of reason and logic in everything. And that included the understanding and treating of psychological disorders. Most clinicians of Freud's time focused on physical factors contributing to mental disorders. As a physician, Freud had been trained in this tradition. But he was struck by the number of his patients suffering from bizarre physical symptoms that had no apparent connection to bodily dysfunction. Building on his work with Jean-Martin Charcot and Josef Breuer, both physicians who were concerned with the links between mind and behavior, Freud set out to look for alternative explanations for the types of psychological disorders he observed in some patients.

Freud became convinced that somatic*—body-related— explanations remained insufficient in understanding and treating these disorders. He began to focus on the unconscious mind, and he used dream interpretation as a creative way to tap into the unconscious. For Freud, the "dream formation touches … problems of psychopathology"*[4] ("psychopathology" here means disorders of the psyche—the mind). Freud relied on both his own dreams and the dreams of his patients in developing this approach. His focus on the psychic rather than the physical, and his creative means of assessing the psychic through dream interpretation remain Freud's most unique contribution in *The Interpretation of Dreams.*

Contribution in Context

Freud was not the first to consider the unconscious mind an important factor in the development of psychological disorders. His work and correspondence with Charcot and Breuer deeply influenced him. Charcot opened Freud's eyes to the notion that some of the behavioral problems he observed could be traced back to past traumas. Indeed, "early psychoanalytic theory … is clearly indebted to Freud's encounter with Charcot."[5] From Charcot, Freud borrowed the idea that events from earlier in life can have lasting effects on the individual—even if the person has no conscious awareness of this.

Breuer treated his patients by talking to them, and this proved very effective. Freud saw this firsthand. It became an important influence as he developed his idea of conducting psychoanalysis by interpreting and analyzing dreams. Breuer believed that recreating "the memory of the incident which eventually led to [hysterical* symptoms] … [could] bring about emotional catharsis by inducing the patient to express any feeling associated with it."[6] "Catharsis" here refers to a purging or release.

Freud modified this therapeutic approach to include interpreting the dream. He found that in describing their dreams, his patients remained less likely to resist discussion of unconscious material that caused them some discomfort: "I have noticed in the course of my psychoanalytic work that the state of mind of a man in contemplation is entirely different from that of a man who is observing his psychic processes … in contemplation one exercises a critique, in consequence of which he rejects some of the ideas which he has perceived … in self-observation, on the other hand, one only has the task of suppressing the critique."[7]

NOTES

1   Sigmund Freud, *The Interpretation of Dreams*, translated by A. A. Brill, with an introduction and notes by Daniel T. O'Hara and Gina Masucci MacKenzie (New York: Barnes & Noble Books, 2005), 13.

2   Freud, *The Interpretation of Dreams*, 13–88.

3   Freud, *The Interpretation of Dreams*, 92–3.

4   Freud, *The Interpretation of Dreams*, 3.

5   K. Libbrecht and J. Quackelbeen, "On the Early History of Male Hysteria and Psychic Trauma. Charcot's influence on Freudian Thought," *Journal of the History of the Behavioral Sciences* 31, no. 4 (1995): 370–84.

6   Richard Webster, "Freud, Charcot, and Hysteria: Lost in the Labyrinth," accessed January 3, 2016, http://www.richardwebster.net/freudandcharcot. html.

7   Freud, *The Interpretation of Dreams*, 93.

SECTION 2
IDEAS

MAIN IDEAS

KEY POINTS

- The central theme in *The Interpretation of Dreams* concerns the notion that dreams contain meaningful information about the sexual and aggressive wishes of the unconscious mind.*

- Freud spends considerable time discussing how the unconscious mind disguises these wishes through the processes of condensation* (compressing several ideas into one element), displacement* (replacing one thing with another), representation* (the way the mind presents concealed thoughts in the content of the dream), and secondary elaboration* (the narrative the unconscious mind provides for what the dream contains).

- Freud's casual writing style and use of specific examples makes his arguments interesting and understandable.

Key Themes

The central idea of Sigmund Freud's *The Interpretation of Dreams* is that dreams contain important information about the desires of the unconscious mind. According to Freud, these desires are often sexual in nature. Freud cited societal views as the key reason the unconscious mind remains so preoccupied with "matters of sex" and with suppressing those impulses. Indeed, he suggests "no other impulse has had to undergo so much suppression from the time of childhood as the sex impulse in its numerous components, from no other impulse have survived so many and such intense unconscious wishes, which now act in the sleeping state in such manner as to produce dreams."[1]

> **❝** The more one is occupied with the solution of dreams, the more willing one must become to acknowledge that the majority of the dreams of adults treat of sexual material and give expression to erotic wishes. **❞**
>
> Sigmund Freud, *The Interpretation of Dreams*

Some people might experience discomfort at recognizing their unconscious sexual urges. Freud believed that portions of the unconscious mind acted as a censor to disguise this sexual material as less offensive by presenting it in dreams. Freud differentiated between a dream's manifest content* (the "story line" presented in the dream) and its latent content* (the dream's true meaning). Freud argued that it is the "latent dream content that far surpasses the manifest dream content in point of significance."[2] In other words, we can only discover the true meaning of the dream after unmasking the disguised wishes of the unconscious and we do this by analyzing and interpreting the dream. For instance, a dream about smoking a cigar might actually reflect some message about the dreamer's preoccupation with male genitalia.

Exploring the Ideas

Freud believed that the unconscious mind actively distorted its wishes. This distortion produced the manifest content of a dream. Specifically, Freud believed this active process of distortion involved four distinct factors: condensation, displacement, representation, and secondary elaboration.

"Condensation" reflects the notion that the mind may compress several different ideas into one single element of a dream's manifest content. As an example, Freud describes the following dream: "I have written a monograph upon a certain plant. The book lies before me, I am just turning over a folded colored plate. A dried specimen of the plant is bound with every copy as though from a herbarium [collection of plant specimens]."[3] In analyzing this dream, Freud asserts that the botanical monograph simultaneously references several things: a previous work he had written about cocaine, a friend of his who uses cocaine in his practice, a patient named Flora, the favorite flowers of his wife, his studies, and his hobbies—and all from a single element of the dream. Freud examined every element of his dream like this, producing a dizzying array of references. In this way he demonstrates that his unconscious chose the elements because "they were able to show the most extensive connections with the dream thoughts, and thus represent nuclei in which a great number of dream thoughts come together."[4]

Freud also believed that the unconscious mind engaged in "displacement." In other words, the contents of the dream might be substitutes for the latent thoughts underlying them. Using the example above, Freud indicated that one of the meanings of his dream reflected his tendency to spend too much money on his hobbies. In this case "the element 'botanical' would in no case find a place in the nucleus of dream thoughts if it were not loosely connected with it by antithesis, for botany was never among my favourite studies."[5] In dreaming of a hobby he did not enjoy, Freud believed that his unconscious was reprimanding him about spending too much money on hobbies that gave him pleasure.

When Freud speaks of "representation," he means the way in which the mind presents latent thoughts in the dream. For Freud, this usually involves some sort of visual imagery. So, for instance, the image of a man atop a tower might represent "the greatness of the man"[6] while an image of a gate "suggests a bodily opening."[7]

The final factor the unconscious mind can use to disguise the latent content of dreams involves "secondary elaboration." Here, Freud argues that the mind smooths out the dream to make its disguised messages less obvious. In other words, the dream receives a cohesive story line that belies the underlying messages and contradictions: "Those parts of the dream with which the secondary elaboration has been able to accomplish something seem to us clear; those where the power of this activity has failed seem confused."[8]

Language and Expression

Providing the reader with relevant background information, Freud offers specific examples that reinforce his argument. While readers may not agree with the conclusions he draws about the nature of the dream, they will finish the work with a greater appreciation of his thought process.

Freud wrote in German, so in talking about the language he used, we must rely on the skill of his various translators. The Austrian psychiatrist* A. A. Brill,* a contemporary of Freud's, produced the first English translation of *The Interpretation of Dreams*. Critics have noted some problems with Brill's work: some of his translations may not be completely accurate and his fluency in English fails him in places.[9] Most of the language remains fairly straightforward, but parts of the text read more formally than modern texts; this reflects some of the idiosyncrasies of Freud's day. For example, he refers to what we commonly call a "wet dream"*—a dream that provokes ejaculation in a man—as a "pollution dream." Context helps to clarify the meaning of most of these references, but they still distract the modern reader unnecessarily. Furthermore, Brill does not translate some references to the work of other scientists and philosophers, so the reader must have some fluency in Spanish, French, and even Latin—or access to a good dictionary—to have any hope of following Freud's point.

NOTES

1   Sigmund Freud, *The Interpretation of Dreams*, translated by A. A. Brill, with an introduction and notes by Daniel T. O'Hara and Gina Masucci MacKenzie (New York: Barnes & Noble Books, 2005), 245.

2   Freud, *The Interpretation of Dreams*, 146.

3   Freud, *The Interpretation of Dreams*, 268.

4   Freud, *The Interpretation of Dreams*, 269.

5   Freud, *The Interpretation of Dreams*, 287.

6   Freud, *The Interpretation of Dreams*, 320.

7   Freud, *The Interpretation of Dreams*, 322.

8   Freud, *The Interpretation of Dreams*, 400.

9   Freud, *The Interpretation of Dreams*, lv.

MODULE 6
SECONDARY IDEAS

KEY POINTS

- Secondary ideas in *The Interpretation of Dreams* include the notion that children experience sexual impulses towards their parents, and a rough theory of mind* (here meaning an attempt to explain the nature and functioning of the mind) outlined in chapter 7.

- These ideas foreshadow Freud's later work on the Oedipus complex* (that is, a child's desire to sleep with the parent of the opposite sex) and Freud's "stage theory" of psychosexual development*—that specific sources of sexual pleasure play a significant role in our individual development towards mental maturity.

- The rough sketch of Freud's theory of the mind provided a foundation for his later ideas about the structure of the mind and personality.*

Other Ideas

Several secondary ideas support the central thesis of Sigmund Freud's *The Interpretation of Dreams.* One is Freud's belief that as a normal part of human development, children develop a sexual attraction toward their parent of the opposite sex. This attraction creates a sense of competition with the parent of the same sex. Freud felt that many symptoms experienced by his neurotic* patients (patients exhibiting symptoms of anxiety in their specific mental condition) stemmed from this complex. He notes that "parents play a leading part in the infantile* [immature] psychology* of all later neurotics."[1] So when children play out the Oedipus complex by falling in love with one parent and hating the other, they lay the groundwork for future mental

> **❝** Perhaps we are all destined to direct our first sexual impulses towards our mothers, and our first hatred and violent wishes towards our fathers; our dreams convince us of it. **❞**
>
> Sigmund Freud, *The Interpretation of Dreams*

health challenges. Or, as Freud put it, they create "that fateful sum of material furnished by the psychic* impulses, which has been formed during the infantile period, and which is of such great importance for the symptoms appearing in the later neurosis."*[2] But, he adds, "I do not think that [neurotics] are here sharply distinguished from normal human beings."[3]

In simple terms, Freud believed everyone has these feelings; neurotics simply display more exaggerated versions of them. In any case, Freud felt analyzing and interpreting dreams would offer insight into these issues.

Another important secondary idea presented in the book involves Freud's theory of the human mind, specifically how the mind operates differently in the waking and the sleeping state. He sees the mind "as a compound instrument, the component parts of which let us call … systems."[4] He describes these systems in the language of the reflex arc,* a popular concept at the time, according to which behavior can be considered a reflexive reaction to sensory input*—sensation. Freud says, "the psychic process generally takes its course from the perception end to the motility end" ("motility" refers to motion).[5] In the case of the dream, however, "the stream of thought is henceforth subjected to a series of transformations which we no longer recognize as normal psychic processes."[6]

In other words, Freud believed that we can only understand the operation of the unconscious mind,* during sleep and dreaming, by careful analysis and interpretation.

Exploring the Ideas

In Freud's view, we all feel sexual and aggressive impulses toward our parents. This fact remains central to some of the sexually motivated wishes of the unconscious mind. To demonstrate the eternal and universal nature of this process, Freud reaches back to ancient Greece and names this phenomenon after one of its most famous tragic figures: Oedipus.* In Freud's recounting of the myth, an oracle tells King Laius* of the city of Thebes that his yet-unborn son will murder him. When his son Oedipus is born, Laius tries to thwart this prophecy by killing the child—or rather, leaving him outside to die. The infant is rescued and taken away to grow up abroad. Later in life, Oedipus "meets King Laius and strikes him dead … and is presented with the hand of Jocasta"*—his mother.[7] Because this myth originated thousands of years earlier, Freud concluded that the Oedipus (or Oedipal) complex occurred frequently. He took this as proof that it must be a normal part of human development.

In chapter 7 of *The Interpretation of Dreams*, Freud presents his theory of the mind. He describes the mind as consisting of multiple systems, or modules. Some of these modules receive sensory information directly and control motor behavior. But Freud's theory also involved less obvious parts of the mind. Indeed, he says that the dream itself "serves as proof for the knowledge of another part of the apparatus."[8] Turning again to the language of reflex ("the motor end") that would be familiar to his readers, he writes that, "the last of the systems at the motor end we call the preconscious* … the system behind it we call the unconscious.*"[9] In other words, Freud believed that a portion of the mind exists between the unconscious and the conscious. This very important idea foreshadows later writings in which he segments the mind into component parts known as the id,* ego,* and superego.* The id is the unconscious center of fundamental impulses such as sexual desire; the ego is the conscious part of the mind in which we form our social identity; the superego is the center of things such as one's sense of conscience* and morality.

In subsequent works, Freud uses the foundation laid in *The Interpretation of Dreams* to elaborate on his stage theory of psychosexual development—the notion that from infancy to maturity we pass through stages in which we derive sexual pleasure from different parts of the body, and that this process can have consequences in later life.

Overlooked

The Interpretation of Dreams brought about significant changes in the way psychiatrists* and psychologists* thought about the mind and the treatment of mental illness. As befits such an influential work, it has received an enormous amount of attention from critics and supporters over the years. So it remains difficult to imagine that any of the ideas of the text have been overlooked.

But we might argue that Freud's work has been somewhat overlooked in the modern world. Indeed, more recent times have seen a "marginalization of psychoanalysis* in psychology textbooks."[10] Freud's ideas have been dismissed because he provides no empirical* evidence to support his claims (that is, no evidence verifiable by observation). This marginalization has accelerated recently as some mental health professionals have shifted their focus about the biological underpinnings of mental illness. We cannot deny that, in general, Freud has left an indelible mark on psychology and the world. But we might argue that modern-day psychologists and psychiatrists have not been greatly influenced by most of the specific ideas he presented in *The Interpretation of Dreams*.[11] However, we have seen renewed interest in some of Freud's ideas among cognitive psychologists* and neuroscientists* (scientists of the brain and nervous system). They remain interested in how we store and access certain types of memory outside our conscious awareness.

NOTES

1   Sigmund Freud, *The Interpretation of Dreams*, translated by A. A. Brill, with an introduction and notes by Daniel T. O'Hara and Gina Masucci MacKenzie (New York: Barnes & Noble Books, 2005), 226.

2   Freud, *The Interpretation of Dreams*, 226.

3   Freud, *The Interpretation of Dreams*, 226.

4   Freud, *The Interpretation of Dreams*, 424.

5   Freud, *The Interpretation of Dreams*, 424.

6   Freud, *The Interpretation of Dreams*, 467.

7   Freud, *The Interpretation of Dreams*, 226–7.

8   Freud, *The Interpretation of Dreams*, 427.

9   Freud, *The Interpretation of Dreams*, 428.

10 Joseph Reppen, "The Relevance of Sigmund Freud for the 21st Century," *Psychoanalytic Psychology* 23, no. 2 (2006): 215–16.

11 Paul R. McHugh, "The Death of Freud and the Rebirth of Psychiatry," *The Weekly Standard*, accessed January 10, 2016, http://www.weeklystandard.com/article/12226.

ACHIEVEMENT

KEY POINTS

- Freud's focus on the role of the unconscious mind* in both neurotics* and healthy individuals has profoundly influenced psychiatry* and psychology* alike.

- Freud's innovative ideas and engaging writing style appealed to a number of other clinicians and led to the establishment of psychoanalysis* as a prominent school of thought.

- The anecdotal nature of Freud's observations (their nature as "stories" applicable to certain individuals alone) and the lack of empirical*—or evidence-based—support for his theories have limited the impact of the ideas Freud introduces in *The Interpretation of Dreams*.

Assessing the Argument

In *The Interpretation of Dreams,* Sigmund Freud hoped to show that the dream serves as a product of the unconscious mind "that knows no other aim in its activity but the fulfillment of wishes."[1] He described the methods of analyzing dreams, noting that this provided a way to gain insight into the unconscious mind. Accessing unconscious thoughts would, Freud felt, give professionals an alternative means of treating various psychological disorders. It would also enhance the dreamer's self-awareness.

Freud based his method in part on the therapeutic approach that he and the Austrian physician Josef Breuer* had described in their *Studies on Hysteria* (1895).[2] In one section of the book, a patient described dreams and engaged in free association* to interpret their true meaning. Freud believed that this process helped a patient's

> ❝ There is no better proof of the great impact Freud has made on psychiatry than the change in its scope, for which his work has been largely responsible. ❞
>
> E. Stengel, "Freud's Impact on Psychiatry"

symptoms to improve, and he reported great success when using the method. He notes that "where it has been possible to trace such a pathological* [that is, diseased] idea back to the elements of the psychic* life of the patient to which it owes its origin, this idea has crumbled away, and the patient has been relieved of it."[3] But the unscientific nature by which Freud arrived at these conclusions would provoke criticism for years to come.

Despite the critics, the ideas Freud introduced in *The Interpretation of Dreams* eventually helped establish psychoanalysis as a prominent perspective in the fields of psychiatry and psychology. In this, Freud achieved his primary aim: he drew attention to the information that dreams give us about the unconscious mind.

Achievement in Context

Freud's concept of the mind was "more profound and more precise"[4] than any of its predecessors, and as such, it appealed to many professionals in the clinical community. It took almost 10 years for the second edition of the book to be published, but over the next few decades *The Interpretation of Dreams* exploded in popularity. In fact, the publisher released six editions between 1910 and 1929 alone.[5]

Many credit Freud with establishing the psychoanalytic perspective in both psychiatry and psychology. This perspective emphasized the role of the unconscious mind in affecting conscious behavior and personality.* It became enormously influential in the early twentieth century. Indeed, one might argue that it remained one of the most prominent perspectives in the field until the mid–twentieth century.[6]

One writer recalls that during his graduate studies, "Freud was prominently studied and psychoanalysts were well represented on faculties of psychology."[7]

The innovative ideas Freud proposed in such interesting ways appealed to many, who became his future disciples. His ideas about the unconscious mind and our ability to access it by interpreting dreams stood in stark contrast to the prominent ideas of the day. The Swiss thinker Carl Jung,* a student of Freud's who became an influential psychiatrist in his own right, suggests "this coinage of a theory marking itself as something extraordinary in the history of science, has a great advantage in that it stands out in bold relief as a strange and unique phenomenon against its philosophical and scientific background."[8] Freud himself recognized his achievement in changing the ways in which the clinical community viewed the unconscious. In his preface to the third edition of the book, he wrote, "the interpretation of dreams was destined to aid in the psychological analysis of the neuroses."[9] Therapists offering Freud's new talk therapy became quite prominent, especially in the United States.

Limitations

Despite its successes, the limitations of *The Interpretation of Dreams* ultimately curtailed its reach and diminished its influence. The modest initial sales of the book disturbed Freud, as they would any author. In his preface to the book's second edition, he writes, "If there has arisen a demand for a second edition … I owe no gratitude to the interest of the professional circles to whom I appealed."[10] However, the increasing frequency of later editions of the book pointed to a surge in interest.

The most fundamental limitations of *The Interpretation of Dreams* concern the ways in which Freud developed his ideas about the unconscious mind. He relied on self-analysis and anecdotal reports in formulating the theory, rather than on systematic, empirical (evidence-based) observations. The ideals of seventeenth- and eighteenth-century intellectual movement known as the Enlightenment* stressed the importance of reason, logic, and scientific inquiry. While his contemporaries upheld these ideals, Freud's anecdotal, unverifiable theory seemed to abandon them. This called into question the validity of Freud's work. Indeed, some viewed Freud as "either an evil-minded villain or someone with a diseased brain pretending that his own delusions* were clinical observations."[11]

NOTES

1   Sigmund Freud, *The Interpretation of Dreams*, translated by A. A. Brill, with an introduction and notes by Daniel T. O'Hara and Gina Masucci MacKenzie (New York: Barnes & Noble Books, 2005), 446.

2   Sigmund Freud and Josef Breuer, *Studies on Hysteria*, trans. James Strachey (London: Hogarth Press, 1955).

3   Freud, *The Interpretation of Dreams*, 92.

4   Ernest Jones, "Freud and His Achievements," *The British Medical Journal* 1, no. 4974 (1956): 997–1000.

5   "Freud's book, 'The Interpretation of Dreams' released 1900," *PBS,* accessed January 24, 2016, http://www.pbs.org/wgbh/aso/databank/entries/dh00fr.html.

6   "Introduction to Psychology," in *Psychology*, 1–34 (Houston, TX: OpenStax College, 2014).

7   Joseph Reppen, "The Relevance of Sigmund Freud for the 21st Century," *Psychoanalytic Psychology* 23, no. 2 (2006): 215–16.

8   C. G. Jung, "Sigmund Freud in His Historical Setting," *Journal of Personality* 1, no. 1 (1932), 48–55.

9   Freud, *The Interpretation of Dreams*, 7.

10 Freud, *The Interpretation of Dreams*, 5.

11 Jones, "Freud and His Achievements," 998.

MODULE 8
PLACE IN THE AUTHOR'S WORK

KEY POINTS

- Freud spent his career describing the importance of the unconscious mind* in behavior and personality,* and he founded the psychoanalytic* school of thought in psychology* and psychiatry.*

- *The Interpretation of Dreams* laid the foundation for Freud's later theories.

- Many consider *The Interpretation of Dreams* one of Freud's most significant achievements. It established his reputation as the father of psychoanalysis.

Positioning

Before Sigmund Freud wrote *The Interpretation of Dreams,* his best-known work had been the 1895 book *Studies on Hysteria*, which he coauthored with the Austrian physician Josef Breuer.*[1] Critics hailed it as a "landmark in psychopathology"* and consider that its publication date marks "the inception of psycho-analysis."[2] In it, Freud and Breuer describe patient case studies and document a unique therapeutic approach. Their new form of "talking therapy"—allowing patients to discuss their issues—was found to relieve a patient's neurotic* symptoms. These outcomes so intrigued Freud that he felt the need to "press forward on the path taken by Breuer until the subject has been fully understood."[3]

Five years later, Freud published *The Interpretation of Dreams*. It reflected ideas he had developed during and after his time with Breuer. Freud had always been fascinated with the role the unconscious mind plays in behavior and personality development. The book's focus on

> ❝ Freud's life-work may be broadly summarized as the exploration of the unconscious after he had devised a method, now known as psycho-analysis for doing so. ❞
>
> Ernest Jones, "Freud and His Achievements"

using dreams to access the wishes of the unconscious mind arose from this interest. *The Interpretation of Dreams* laid a foundation for much of the rest of his professional work. Several ideas it introduced foreshadowed Freud's later writings about both his theory of mind* (his theory of the nature, structure, and functioning of the mind) and his "stage theory" of psychosexual development,* according to which we achieve psychic* maturity from infancy by passing through various stages in which we derive sexual pleasure from different bodily sources.

Integration

Throughout his career as a psychoanalyst, Freud believed that to understand human behavior and personality, one must understand the wishes of the unconscious mind. All Freud's work centers on this concept, using *The Interpretation of Dreams* as a foundation. In *The Interpretation of Dreams*, Freud presented a rough, reflex-like sketch of the mind. In later works, he outlined "a 'topography' of the psyche* in three parts: the id,* the ego,* and the super-ego.*"[4] These he identified as divisions of the unconscious mind: together, they contain all the desires and wishes an individual's mind has suppressed. Freud believed that most of those desires remained sexual in nature. The ego essentially represents the conscious mind.* It is "sandwiched between the id and super-ego."[5] The superego represents the sense of conscience.* The id represents the sexual and aggressive impulses of the unconscious mind. According to Freud, the ego remains in a constant state of tension trying to balance the demands of both the id and the superego.

In *The Interpretation of Dreams,* Freud hints at another major theory to come. In describing the sexual and aggressive impulses that children feel toward their parents, Freud references the story of the mythical Greek King Oedipus.* This story found a place in his later works, when Freud proposes a stage theory of psychosexual development. One of these stages includes the phenomenon Freud named the "Oedipus complex."* He sees this as a normal part of every person's development. Briefly, the stage theory of psychosexual development describes development migrating through erogenous zones* (places in which sexual pleasure is to be gained) in a growing child's body.

Freud associates each zone with a series of conflicts; people who fail to successfully resolve these conflicts develop fixations* (excessive preoccupations) that affect their personality and behavior. For example, one of the earliest stages involves the erogenous zone centering on the mouth. This would correlate to early in an infant's life, when it relies on suckling to survive. If the mother weaned the child too soon or too late, an oral fixation could develop. Accordingly, "an adult who smokes, drinks, overeats, or bites [their] nails"[6] would be assumed to suffer from an oral fixation. As time goes on, the erogenous zone moves from the mouth to the anus and then on to the genitals or phallus (the period when the Oedipus complex occurs). After the phallic stage, a period of relative inactivity ensues. Then, about the time of puberty, the erogenous zone becomes centered on the genitals and remains there for the rest of the individual's life.

Significance

A prolific writer, Sigmund Freud published more than 300 works over the course of his career. Yet he often identified *The Interpretation of Dreams* as his personal favorite.[7] Indeed, "the preface to the third English edition (1931) of *The Interpretation of Dreams* makes clear the place of this book in the eye of its author: '[This book] contains … the most valuable of all the discoveries it has been my good fortune to make. Insight such as this falls to one's lot but once in a lifetime.'"[8] Both supporters and critics share this view, routinely citing "the centrality of the dream book to psychoanalysis."[9] Supporters have levied "laudatory epithets [that is, admiring descriptions], with [the German American historian] Peter Gay* comparing it to [the foundational evolutionary theorist] Charles Darwin's* *On the Origin of Species* as a 'revolutionary classic shaping modern culture.'"[10]

Earlier in his career, Freud published on topics ranging from a historical and clinical study of cocaine to a study of cerebral paralysis (paralysis of the brain) in children.[11] After *The Interpretation of Dreams*, his work followed one direction as he continued to elaborate on many of the ideas he introduced in his masterwork. *The Interpretation of Dreams* represented Freud's "magnum opus [masterpiece] … which was the foundation of all his later work."[12] While Freud's influence has waned in the last few decades, that does not diminish the central role this text played in his career.

NOTES

1   Sigmund Freud and Josef Breuer, *Studies on Hysteria*, trans. James Strachey (London: Hogarth Press, 1955).

2   Ernest Jones, "Freud and His Achievements," *The British Medical Journal* 1, no. 4974 (1956): 997–1000.

3   Sigmund Freud, *The Interpretation of Dreams*, translated by A. A. Brill, with an introduction and notes by Daniel T. O'Hara and Gina Masucci MacKenzie (New York: Barnes & Noble Books, 2005), 92.

4   Paul Ricoeur, "Sigmund Freud," in Karl Simms, *Paul Ricoeur: Routledge Critical Thinkers* (Abingdon, UK: Taylor & Francis, 2002), 46.

5   Ricoeur, "Sigmund Freud," 46.

6   "Personality," in *Psychology*, 369–410 (Houston, TX: OpenStax College, 2014), 375.

7   Kendra Cherry, "Books by Sigmund Freud: Freud's Most Famous and Influential Books," accessed January 9, 2016, http://psychology.about.com/od/sigmundfreud/tp/books-by-sigmund-freud.htm.

8   Patricia Kitcher, *Freud's Dream: A Complete Interdisciplinary Science of Mind* (Cambridge, MA: MIT Press, 1992), 113.

9   Kitcher, *Freud's Dream*, 113.

10 Kitcher, *Freud's Dream*, 113.

11 Jones, "Freud and His Achievements," 997–1000.

12 Jones, "Freud and His Achievements," 999.

SECTION 3
IMPACT

THE FIRST RESPONSES

KEY POINTS

- Freud's emphasis on infantile* sexuality and his nonscientific approach served as fodder for early critics.

- Freud ignored some criticism, but when former colleagues started criticizing his work, he often cut off contact with them.

- How readers received the text largely depended on their personal convictions and their loyalty to Freud.

Criticism

Critics largely ignored Sigmund Freud's *The Interpretation of Dreams* in the first few years after its publication because it did not accord with the common scientific themes of the time but its popularity grew. As Freud's ideas gained momentum, he found himself at the head of a new school of thought in the psychiatric* and psychological* communities: the psychoanalytic* movement. The First International Congress of Psychoanalysis convened in 1908 and a group of psychoanalysts established the International Psychoanalytical Association two years later. Freud became something of a celebrity. He and his student, the Swiss psychoanalyst Carl Jung,* traveled to the United States, lecturing on psychoanalysis.[1]

Despite all this acclaim, the book also generated controversy and criticism. Freud's critics took issue with the speculative nature of his ideas and the subjectivity involved in developing them. Seeing these as major flaws, critics questioned the scientific value of Freud's work. Some merely distanced themselves from Freud; others openly criticized his ideas.

> ❝ The Freudian theory … is at best a partial truth, and therefore in order to maintain itself and be effective, it has the rigidity of a dogma and the fanaticism of an inquisitor. ❞
>
> Carl Jung, "Sigmund Freud in His Historical Setting"

Josef Breuer,* Freud's collaborator on *Studies on Hysteria* (1895), both distanced himself and criticized Freud. Indeed, scholars have traditionally assumed that he severed all ties with Freud "because Breuer objected to Freud's claim that there was a sexual etiology* for the psychoneuroses."[*2] ("Etiology" refers to the causes of a disease.) Others have claimed that the two broke off relations because "Breuer … could not tolerate such an affront to rationalism"* inherent in Freud's ideas.[3]

Breuer was not the only person in Freud's life who switched from colleague to critic. Carl Jung, one of Freud's students, also turned into a fierce critic. "The dynamic that developed between them was one where, having first declared Jung his 'heir apparent,' Freud would go on to call him 'mad' six years later."[4] This separation occurred when Jung took exception to Freud's ideas about the importance of sexual impulses and early childhood experiences in determining adult behavior. Jung countered that human goals and aspirations also serve as important motivating forces. Jung considered Freud's ideas about the unconscious mind* underdeveloped. While his view of the personal unconscious was very similar to Freud's, Jung identified an extra layer of the unconscious mind, which he called the "collective unconscious"[*5]—a part of the unconscious mind shared or contributed to by everyone. Another factor differentiating Jung from his former mentor is his treatment of religion and spirituality. Jung placed these in the collective unconscious.[6]

Responses

Describing Freud's response to his critics, one writer notes that he "bore all this hostility with considerable fortitude and never deigned to reply to it in public; in private, he even derived a certain amount of amusement … I remember his remarking once: 'My opponents may abuse my doctrines by day, but I am sure they dream of them by night.'"[7] This aloof approach did little to abate the criticism. Indeed, to this day critics continue to raise many of the same objections about the unscientific nature of Freud's theories.

Freud could use humor to distance himself from some opponents, but criticism from colleagues who had once been his closest allies wounded him deeply. Freud felt personally betrayed and hurt by Jung's criticism. What had begun as a great friendship steeped in mutual respect transformed into a fierce rivalry. Jung and Freud's correspondence became increasingly hostile; eventually they stopped communicating altogether. Indeed, in his last letter to Jung, Freud wrote, "I propose that we abandon our personal relationship entirely. I shall lose nothing by it, for my only emotional tie with you has long been a thin thread."[8] As a consequence, Freud began isolate himself from his critics. Instead, he surrounded himself with a close-knit group of colleagues who fiercely defended the principles of psychoanalysis.[9]

Conflict and Consensus

Freud and his critics could not agree on much, and these disagreements continued for many years. Jung and Breuer were not the only former colleagues who felt Freud's professional and personal wrath. He also broke with the Austrian physician and psychotherapist Alfred Adler* and the Hungarian psychoanalyst Sándor Ferenczi,* both of whom were former students of his. Ernest Jones,* a psychoanalyst who supported Freud to the end, says Adler and Ferenczi became unable "to face the conclusions that follow from deep psycho-analytic investigation … [They] turned away and repudiated the conclusions they had once accepted and expounded."[10] However, Jones admits that like Adler and Jung, many critics "were able to enjoy successful careers on the basis of rejecting Freud's sexual theories, and the general public welcomed them with a sense of relief at being rescued from Freud's displeasing ideas."[11]

In the end, reactions to Freud's *The Interpretation of Dreams* depended largely on personal convictions and loyalties. Some, like Jones, remained incredibly loyal; in fact, Jones went on to become Freud's biographer. Theorists like Jung accepted many of the doctrines Freud set out, but modified them in ways that matched their own ideas about the nature of the unconscious mind. Breuer and others dismissed Freud's ideas outright. They objected to the unscientific way in which he constructed his theories of the unconscious mind and dream analysis.*

NOTES

1   Sigmund Freud, *The Interpretation of Dreams*, translated by A. A. Brill, with an introduction and notes by Daniel T. O'Hara and Gina Masucci MacKenzie (New York: Barnes & Noble Books, 2005), xv.

2   John P. Muller, "A Re-Reading of *Studies on Hysteria*: The Freud-Breuer Break Revisited," *Psychoanalytic Psychology* 9, no. 2 (1992): 129–56.

3   Muller, "A Re-Reading of *Studies on Hysteria*," 129.

4   Hester McFarland Solomon, "Freud and Jung: An Incomplete Encounter," *Journal of Analytical Psychology* 48, no. 5 (2003): 553–69.

5   Kendra Cherry, "Sigmund Freud Photobiography: Freud and Jung," accessed January 9, 2016, http://psychology.about.com/od/sigmundfreud/ig/Sigmund-Freud-Photobiography/Freud-and-Jung.htm.

6   "The Well-Documented Friendship of Carl Jung and Sigmund Freud," Historacle.org, accessed January 9, 2016, http://historacle.org/freud_jung.html.

7   Ernest Jones, "Freud and His Achievements," *The British Medical Journal* 1, no. 4974 (1956): 997–1000.

8   David Eidenberg, "Freud and Jung: A 'Psychoanalysis' in Letters," *Psychological Perspectives* 57 (2014): 7–24.

9   Cherry, "Sigmund Freud Photobiography: Freud and Jung."

10 Jones, "Freud and His Achievements," 998.

11 Jones, "Freud and His Achievements," 998.

THE EVOLVING DEBATE

KEY POINTS

- *The Interpretation of Dreams* helped establish psychoanalysis* as both a therapeutic technique and a school of thought.

- Psychodynamic* approaches (those approaches linking the unconscious mind* and conscious behavior) like the analytical perspective* owe their establishment to the works of Freud.

- Scholars consider *The Interpretation of Dreams* Freud's greatest work; it remains core reading for anyone trying to better understand the basic principles of psychoanalysis.

Uses and Problems

Many critics dismissed Sigmund Freud's *The Interpretation of Dreams*. They felt he "had exaggerated the role of sexuality, relied on faulty methods, and succumbed to wild speculation."[1] However, his supporters recognized—and continue to recognize—the enormous impact his work has had on both psychiatry* and psychology.*

The Interpretation of Dreams laid the foundation for the psychoanalytic perspective and established Freud as the unquestioned leader of the psychoanalytic movement. Freud's perspective created a new way of thinking—"a cultural revolution comparable in scope to that unleashed by [the English naturist and evolutionary theorist Charles] Darwin.*"[2] It also offered a new therapeutic technique for professionals. Soon, psychiatrists began to treat people with various mental illnesses by using therapies involving dream analysis* and free association.*[3]

> **❝** Freud has not only expanded the range of
> psychiatry, he has also given it new dimensions
> in depth by the discovery and exploration of the
> dynamic unconscious—that is, of mental forces which
> influence behaviour and which can be brought into
> consciousness.* **❞**
>
> E. Stengel, "Freud's Impact on Psychiatry"

Freud remained fiercely protective of the key tenets of his theories. He especially insisted on the role the sexual impulse plays in fueling the desires of the unconscious mind. This idea remained central to him. Freud's rigid adherence to his ideas created tensions with some of his strongest supporters, a number of whom wanted to modify the concept of the unconscious. Freud's former student Carl Jung* and others eventually founded their own related schools of thought. Derived from Freudian principles, they became collectively known as neo-Freudians* and developed distinguished careers in their own right.

Schools of Thought

The psychoanalytical perspective born of Freud's work emphasized the ways in which the unconscious mind affects behavior and personality.* Freud viewed the unconscious mind as a reservoir of unfulfilled wishes and impulses. People express their unconscious sexual wishes in dreams. In fact, in his view, most of the psychic* energy tied up in the unconscious mind directly results from sexual impulses being forced out of conscious awareness by some censor mechanism. Freud would later name this internal censor the "superego"*—the part of the mind governing morality and our unconscious instincts. Freud held that we can only truly understand these unconscious wishes by engaging in the processes of dream analysis and interpretation.[4]

As happens with any innovator, not all of Freud's followers accepted all of his ideas. Some of these disagreements led to the development of alternate schools of thought. Scholars credit Freud's student-turned-critic Carl Jung with establishing the analytical perspective—an alternative school of thought to psychoanalysis. Jung emphasized his own unique ideas about the collective unconscious*— the part of the unconscious mind we share with others—and its shared images and patterns, which he called "archetypes."* Unlike Freud, Jung also applied many of his ideas to religion and spirituality.[5] Jung might have remained a supporter of Freud had his teacher been open to modifying his approach. However, "in expecting that Jung, as his adept and chosen heir, would display uncritical devotion to the theory of psychoanalysis that he had conceived, Freud had badly misjudged the younger psychiatrist."[6]

In Current Scholarship

Today's scholars often group the psychoanalytic and analytical perspectives together with others under the heading of "psychodynamic" approaches. The psychodynamic perspective refers to "all the theories in psychology that see human functioning based upon the interaction of drives and forces within the person, particularly unconscious, and between the different structures of the personality."[7] While the influence of psychoanalysis in particular has waned in recent years, many mental health professionals still follow the therapeutic approaches put forward by Freud and his followers, the neo-Freudians. Anyone who wants to understand this perspective would be wise to read this critical text. One clinician noted that she "cannot be a fully 'Jungian analyst' without having an intimate knowledge of and without pursuing in depth my study of the foundations and theoretical developments of 'Freudian psychoanalysis.'"[8]

Outside clinical circles, people still discuss *The Interpretation of Dreams* and Freud's other works widely. But these discussions generally focus on historical value and influence. Still, new advances in cognitive neuroscience*—scientific investigation into the process of thought—may open the door to a more prominent role for Freud's works today. One author notes that "within the context of certain psychiatric and neuroscientific* circles, psychoanalysis has become a topic of renewed interest."[9] Indeed, scholars resumed defending "the potential legitimacy of psychoanalytic theory and practice"[10] as early as the mid-1980s.

NOTES

1   Anthony D. Kaunders, "Truth, Truthfulness, and Psychoanalysis: The Reception of Freud in Wilhelmine Germany," *German History* 31, no. 1 (2013): 1–22.

2   Henri F. Ellenberger, *The Discovery of the Unconscious: The History and Evolution of Dynamic Psychiatry* (New York: Basic Books, 2008), 418.

3   Ernest Jones, "Freud and His Achievements," *The British Medical Journal* 1, no. 4974 (1956): 997–1000.

4   Saul McLeod, "Psychodynamic Approach," *Simply Psychology,* accessed January 10, 2016, http://www.simplypsychology.org/psychodynamic.html.

5   McLeod, "Psychodynamic Approach."

6   Hester McFarland Solomon, "Freud and Jung: An Incomplete Encounter," *Journal of Analytical Psychology* 48, no. 5 (2003): 554.

7   McLeod, "Psychodynamic Approach."

8   Solomon, "Freud and Jung," 553–69.

9   Nima Bassiri, "Freud and the Matter of the Brain: On the Rearrangements of Neuropsychoanalysis," *Critical Inquiry* 40, no. 1 (2013): 83–108.

10 Bassiri, "Freud and the Matter of the Brain," 83.

IMPACT AND INFLUENCE TODAY

KEY POINTS

- While *The Interpretation of Dreams* has become less relevant for today's mental health professionals, it remains a classic text still capable of capturing the interests of modern-day psychologists.*

- Freud's insistence on the importance of the unconscious* brought into focus the unconscious aspects of the mind and has left an indelible mark on the history of psychology.

- Lively debate continues about the relevance of Freud's ideas in the twenty-first century. Some relegate his ideas to the annals of history and others point to the potential value that these ideas still hold.

Position

Sigmund Freud's *The Interpretation of Dreams* ushered in the psychoanalytic* movement. "[From] 1935 to 1975 … Freudianism was the unchallenged doctrine of American psychiatry.*"[1] One writer lamented that "recent discoveries in biomedicine,* which the public may think are great advances, have in fact plucked the 'soul' from psychiatry,* leaving it a cold business that dispenses magical pills rather than addressing patients in all their tragic peculiarity."[2] ("Biomedical" approaches to mental health are based on the treatment of the physical organism, routinely conducted with medicine.) Others suggest that this change allows psychiatry to "grow as a science-based, evidence-driven discipline."[3]

Today, mental health professionals use a range of therapeutic approaches. Psychoanalysts still offer their services, but their numbers—and their influence—have steadily declined. Indeed, it has

> **❝** In their disciplinary merger, it has been argued, psychoanalysis and the neurosciences could directly benefit one another; the neurosciences could be infused with a more robust theory of subjective experience while psychoanalysis could make the transition to becoming a testable, experimental science. **❞**
>
> Nima Bassiri, "Freud and the Matter of the Brain: On the Rearrangements of Neuropsychoanalysis"

been claimed that "the number of publishers willing to publish psychoanalytic titles has decreased dramatically … the major university presses are no longer willing even to consider psychoanalytic titles."[4]

Some have attributed this shift in attitude to "the biological turn in psychiatry and emergence of cognitive neurosciences* as the dominant paradigm in psychology [departments] and journals around the world."[5] Cognitive neurosciences examine thought in the light of the electrical and chemical functioning of the physical brain. Although this once seemed a death knell for psychoanalysis, it may become an opportunity for its rebirth. As the interest in neuroscience "has grown steadily in the last decades, configuring a well-developed field of knowledge … some of its practitioners have paid increasing attention to areas of inquiry within, or close to, the realm of psychoanalytical interest."[6] Psychoanalysis and neuroscience could potentially work together, with possible opportunities for joint investigation involving such concepts as memories that exist outside conscious awareness.

Interaction

Not everyone feels enthusiastic about the idea of merging psychoanalysis and neuroscience. In fact, many in the psychoanalytic camp have resisted it, considering psychoanalysis "a 'nonscientific field' of knowledge, linked to humanities* and far from natural sciences.*"[7] The "humanities" is a broad area of scholarship including the studies of history, literature, and culture, and so by linking psychoanalysis with neuroscience, some feel that its very foundation would become threatened.

However, the field of psychoanalysis remains quite splintered. Indeed, it has been argued that, "a multitude of groups and factions … debate the true heritage of the Freudian legacy, and unfortunately dedicate insufficient time and effort to improving teaching and research methods."[8] As a result, "psychoanalysts have disappeared from the academic frontline in many countries, especially in the United States, where they once occupied privileged positions in many departments."[9]

A number of psychoanalysts have even begun to question the relevance of Freud's ideas in the twenty-first century. One writer notes, "there are 'two Freuds' … Freud, the natural scientist,* and Freud the hermeneutist."[10] A hermeneutist is someone who specializes in interpretation—in other words, we may think of Freud as both a physician and an expert in interpretation, and specifically in interpreting the individual's unfulfilled wishes as expressed in dreams. The writer quoted above argues that to determine the relevance of Freud's arguments, we must examine them on a case-by-case basis.

The Continuing Debate

Neuroscientists may begin to examine memories stored in the unconscious mind. Many psychoanalysts welcome this possibility. Applying psychoanalytic principles in the context of neuroscience allows us to "study the physical support for mental life, which helps us complement and refine our ideas, and in addition allows us to offer models and concepts that may enrich the research of biologists."[11] In other words, today's technology can show us how unconscious processes produce activity in the brain.

However, neuroscientists will investigate these ideas in very different ways than their psychoanalyst colleagues. As one writer has asserted, "Freud's biologically based constructs … are not relevant for the twenty-first century … [As] it turns out psychoanalysts have begun to view the effects of biology on psychological reactions, but a biology based on neuroscience and the structures of the brain, not the neurophysiology* of the functioning of the nerves and inherited content of the mind, that guided Freud's thinking."[12] "Neurophysiology" here refers to the physical structure and functioning of the brain and nervous system.

Still, neuroscience may offer an unanticipated lifeline to psychoanalysis. Unless it establishes its relevance for today, the discipline will fall victim to "its own inevitable obsolescence, a consequence of its inability or refusal to evolve as a natural, experimental science."[13] We may note some irony here: in establishing psychoanalysis, Freud, who trained as a medical doctor, decided to forego scientific methods of testing and verification. He relied instead on anecdotes and personal observation. However, if psychoanalysis is to remain relevant, it must now rely on science.

NOTES

1 Paul R. McHugh, "The Death of Freud and the Rebirth of Psychiatry," *The Weekly Standard,* accessed January 10, 2016, http://www.weeklystandard.com/article/12226.

2 McHugh, "The Death of Freud and the Rebirth of Psychiatry."

3 McHugh, "The Death of Freud and the Rebirth of Psychiatry."

4 Carlo Strenger, "Can Psychoanalysis Reclaim the Public Sphere?," *Psychoanalytic Psychology* 32, no. 2 (2015): 293–306.

5 Strenger, "Can Psychoanalysis Reclaim the Public Sphere?," 294.

6 Miguel Angel Gonzalez-Torres, "Psychoanalysis and Neuroscience. Friends or Enemies?" *International Forum of Psychoanalysis* 22, no. 1 (2013): 35–42.

7   Gonzalez-Torres, "Psychoanalysis and Neuroscience," 36.

8   Gonzalez-Torres, "Psychoanalysis and Neuroscience," 37.

9   Gonzalez-Torres, "Psychoanalysis and Neuroscience," 37.

10   George Frank, "A Response to 'The Relevance of Sigmund Freud for the 21st Century,'" *Psychoanalytic Psychology* 25, no. 2 (2008): 375–9.

11   Gonzalez-Torres, "Psychoanalysis and Neuroscience," 38.

12   Frank, "A Response," 376.

13   Nima Bassiri, "Freud and the Matter of the Brain: On the Rearrangements of Neuropsychoanalysis," *Critical Inquiry* 40, no. 1 (2013): 83–108.

WHERE NEXT?

KEY POINTS

- The best future potential for *The Interpretation of Dreams* lies in the ways it can support neuropsychoanalytic* interests (neuropsychoanalysis is the term used to describe the merging of psychoanalytic* and neuroscience* perspectives; neuroscience is the scientific study of the brain and nervous system).

- *The Interpretation of Dreams* will continue to serve as an important part of the history of both psychology* and psychiatry.*

- *The Interpretation of Dreams* remains one of the core— and most influential—texts in both psychology and psychiatry.

Potential

Sigmund Freud's *The Interpretation of Dreams* has shaped unique schools of thought in the fields of psychology and psychiatry. In this sense, it has already achieved its full potential. Psychoanalysis remained a dominant perspective in psychology for several decades, its influence perhaps most apparent in the United States. Since the mid-1970s, the numbers—and influence—of psychoanalysts have declined significantly. As pharmacological treatments of various psychological disorders have become available, interest has shifted to more evidence-based forms of therapy (pharmacology is the science of drugs).[1] It remains difficult to imagine any future situation in which psychoanalysis might regain its tremendous influence. But *The Interpretation of Dreams* will certainly retain its place as one of the classic texts in both fields. Practitioners and lay readers will continue to study it for its significant historical value.

> ❝ My purpose … is to suggest one way that psychoanalysis might re-energize itself, and that is by developing a closer relationship with biology in general and with cognitive neuroscience in particular. ❞
>
> Eric R. Kandel, "Biology and the Future of Psychoanalysis: A New Intellectual Framework for Psychiatry Revisited"

That said, neuroscientists trying to better understand the mind have renewed their interest in some of Freud's psychoanalytic ideas. This has led to an increased number of calls to merge the two disciplines into the new field of neuropsychoanalysis.* This discipline has attracted some significant support. The Nobel Prize-winning neuropsychiatrist* Eric Kandel* said, "it is my hope that by joining with cognitive neuroscience* in developing a new and compelling perspective on the mind and its disorders, psychoanalysis will regain its intellectual energy."[2] Such a merger may represent the best future potential for Freud's ideas.

Future Directions

In a 1999 paper, Kandel laid out a framework for the future of neuropsychoanalysis. "Central to psychoanalysis," Kandel writes, "is the idea that we are unaware of much of our mental life."[3] Neuroscientists already make distinctions between explicit (conscious) memories* and implicit or procedural memories.* "Procedural" here relates to unconscious memories such as those concerning the performance of processes such as tasks.

Neuropsychoanalysts might map these distinctions onto the psychoanalytic view of the mind. Kandel points out that "one of the earlier limitations to the study of unconscious psychic* processes was that no method existed for directly observing them." But "a key contribution that biology can now make—with its ability to image mental processes and its ability to study patients with lesions in different components of procedural memory—is to change the basis of the study of the unconscious mental processes from indirect inference to direct observation."[4]

Kandel notes that some of the techniques Freud used, such as free association,* also lend themselves to biological study. "[We] have in biology a good beginning of an understanding of how associations develop in procedural memory … insofar as aspects of procedural knowledge are relevant to moments of meaning, these biological insights should prove useful for understanding the procedural unconscious."[5] He sees further potential convergences between the psychoanalytic and neuroscience perspectives. These include the links between thoughts and psychopathology,* the role that early experiences play in psychopathology, and the role played by the part of the brain known as the prefrontal cortex,* associated with higher cognitive functioning, in preconscious* thought. "Preconscious" here refers to the part of the mind that exists between the unconscious and the conscious; memories the mind does not suppress exist here before they are called into consciousness.*

Summary

Sigmund Freud's *The Interpretation of Dreams* remains a classic text in the fields of both psychology and psychiatry. We cannot overstate the impact that Freud, this important book, and the subsequent rise of the psychoanalytic school of thought have had in these areas. Kandel sums it up well when he writes, "During the first half of the twentieth century, psychoanalysis revolutionized our understanding of mental life. It provided a remarkable set of new insights about unconscious mental processes."[6] Scholars have compared Freud's genius to that of the English evolutionary scholar Charles Darwin* and the German physicist Albert Einstein.* Although Freud wrote prolifically, scholars have identified *The Interpretation of Dreams* as his single most important work.[7] Any reader interested in the history of psychology and psychiatry, in neuroscience, or in the ways Freud has influenced the culture at large would benefit from reading *The Interpretation of Dreams*. And as neuroscientists renew their interest in psychoanalytic principles, this text should remain relevant for years to come.

There will always be new insights to gain—indeed, many concepts of the unconscious mind* have changed in the last few decades. But *The Interpretation of Dreams* sets forth one of the most famous and influential theories of mind* ever proposed. While its relevance may have changed since Freud's day, its significance is assured.

NOTES

1   Paul R. McHugh, "The Death of Freud and the Rebirth of Psychiatry," *The Weekly Standard,* accessed January 10, 2016, http://www.weeklystandard.com/article/12226.

2   Eric R. Kandel, "Biology and the Future of Psychoanalysis: A New Intellectual Framework for Psychiatry Revisited," *The American Journal of Psychiatry* 156, no. 4 (1999): 505–24.

3   Kandel, "Biology and the Future of Psychoanalysis," 508.

4   Kandel, "Biology and the Future of Psychoanalysis," 510.

5   Kandel, "Biology and the Future of Psychoanalysis," 510.

6   Kandel, "Biology and the Future of Psychoanalysis," 505.

7   Patricia Kitcher, *Freud's Dream: A Complete Interdisciplinary Science of Mind* (Cambridge, MA: MIT Press, 1992).

GLOSSARY

GLOSSARY OF TERMS

Analytical perspective: an alternative school of thought to psychoanalysis founded by Freud's student Carl Jung.

Anti-Semitism: prejudice targeting Jewish people.

Archetype: in this context, refers to the images and patterns that occur in the collective unconscious (a term coined by the psychoanalyst Carl Jung for the part of the unconscious mind shared among populations or communities).

Biomedicine: the application of biological principles in medicine.

Collective unconscious: Jung's concept of the part of the unconscious mind all people share.

Condensation: in this context, the compression of several ideas into one element of the manifest (obvious) dream content.

Cognitive neuroscience: a branch of neuroscience that studies behavior and thought processes in terms of the biological functions of the brain.

Cognitive psychology: the study of the human mind and behavior as it relates to thought.

Conscience: one's sense of right and wrong.

Consciousness: one's state of awareness.

Defenses (ego defense mechanisms): unconscious techniques for dealing with anxiety.

Delusion: a false belief.

Displacement: in this context, substitutions made in the latent (concealed and "true") and manifest (describable) content of dreams.

Dream analysis: in this context, a process that uses free association to determine the meaning of a dream.

Ego: according to Freud, the part of the conscious mind that operates between the id and the superego.

Enlightenment: a seventeenth- and eighteenth-century cultural, intellectual, and philosophical movement that emphasized social and personal progress through education, science, individualism, and reason.

Empirical: based on observable evidence.

Erogenous zone: according to Freud, the area of the body in which sexual energy is centered. This zone moves through various areas as a person develops.

Explicit memory: memories a person is consciously aware of and can recall.

Etiology: the reason something occurs.

Fixation: persistent focus on an erogenous zone that was unsuccessfully resolved during psychosexual development.

Free association: an exercise in which one person (the therapist, for instance) says a word and the other (the patient) responds immediately with another word. There may be no obvious connection between the two words.

Freudian slip: a mistake in speech that is thought to reveal something about the individual's unconscious wishes.

Humanities: disciplines in academia that focus on human culture.

Hypnosis: a procedure in which a person experiences an altered state of consciousness that renders him or her especially open to the power of suggestion.

Hysteria: in this context, a neurotic disorder characterized by extreme emotion and altered sensory/motor function.

Id: a reservoir of unconscious impulses and psychic energy.

Inertia: in this context, a discharge of excess excitation in the nervous system.

Infantile: relating to infants.

Latent content: the true meaning of a dream.

Manifest content: a dream's story line.

Materialism: in this context, the assumption that all mental processes are a function of the brain.

Motor output: signals sent to muscles from the nervous system that cause the body to move or act.

Natural science: academic disciplines concerned with understanding the natural world.

Nazi Germany (1933–1945): the period when Adolf Hitler and his Nazi Party ruled Germany and, during the course of World War II, several other countries as well. Fiercely anti-Semitic, the Nazis would eventually imprison and execute six million Jews, homosexuals, and others they considered "undesirable."

Neo-Freudians: a label used to describe theorists and therapists influenced by Freud but who took exception to some of his specific assertions about psychoanalysis.

Neural activity: activity in the cells of the brain.

Neurologist: a doctor specializing in the treatment of diseases of the nervous system and brain.

Neuropathology: the branch of medicine that deals with diseases of the nervous system.

Neurophysiology: study of the function of the nervous system.

Neuropsychiatry: the study of the role of the nervous system in disorders of the mind.

Neuropsychoanalysis: the term used to describe a merging of psychoanalytic and neuroscience perspectives.

Neuroscience: an interdisciplinary area concerned with studying the structure and function of the nervous system.

Neurosis (psychoneurosis): mental illness involving anxiety.

Neurotics: patients exhibiting symptoms of anxiety in their specific mental condition.

Obsession: pronounced preoccupation with some idea, often associated with anxiety.

Oedipus complex: Freud's idea that normal development involves developing (and eventually suppressing) sexual impulses toward the opposite-sex parent while viewing the other parent as a threat.

Pathological: related to disease.

Personality: an individual's characteristic pattern of thought and behavior.

Phobia: an intense, irrational fear.

Preconscious: the part of the mind that exists between the unconscious and the conscious. Memories the mind does not suppress exist here before they are called into consciousness.

Prefrontal cortex: an area of the brain associated with higher cognitive functions.

Procedural memory: memory of how to engage in tasks; often a person does not consciously recall this memory.

Projection: a Freudian ego defense mechanism by which an individual attributes his or her own uncomfortable thoughts to someone else.

Psyche: the mind.

Psychiatry: a branch of medicine involved in treating psychological disorders.

Psychic: in this context, concerning mental processes.

Psychoanalysis: a school of thought emphasizing the role the unconscious mind plays in conscious behavior; also a therapeutic approach that employs various techniques to try to access the unconscious mind.

Psychodynamic: a school of thought that emphasizes that unconscious forces shape behavior.

Psychology: the scientific study of mental processes and behaviors.

Psychoneurosis (also neurosis): mental illness involving anxiety.
Psychopathology: the study of the diseases of the mind.

Rationalism: a philosophical perspective emphasizing reason and logic.

Rationalization: a Freudian ego defense mechanism in which an individual tries to justify his or her behavior by explaining it.

Reflex arc: a popular concept in Freud's time, according to which behavior can be considered a reflexive reaction to sensory input or sensation.

Reflex circuits: neural circuits involving sensory input and motor output.

Representation: in this context, refers to the way the mind presents latent thoughts in the manifest content of the dream.

Repression: a Freudian ego defense mechanism that involves pushing uncomfortable thoughts and memories out of conscious awareness.

Secondary elaboration: the cohesive narrative the unconscious mind provides for the dream's manifest content.

Sensory input: information received by sensory receptors that is then transmitted to the brain.

Stage theory of psychosexual development: Freud's ideas that the resolution of conflicts center on the location of an individual's erogenous zones at a given period in development. Resolving—or not resolving—these conflicts has long-term consequences for the individual's personality.

Superego: the part of the mind that contains one's sense of conscience.

Theory of mind: Freud's attempt to explain the thought processes that occur in other people.

Unconscious mind: the portion of the mind that falls outside conscious awareness.

Victorian era: a specific period of history (roughly marked by the reign of Great Britain's Queen Victoria) from the nineteenth into the early twentieth century. Most importantly here, Victorians had a moral preoccupation with sexuality.

Wet dream: a dream that involves ejaculation.

PEOPLE MENTIONED IN THE TEXT

Alfred Adler (1870–1937) was an Austrian physician and psychotherapist. A former follower of Freud, Adler went on to found individual psychology.

Josef Breuer (1842–1925) was an Austrian physician who mentored Freud and collaborated with him on *Studies on Hysteria*.

A. A. Brill (1874–1948) was an Austrian psychiatrist who was the first to translate *The Interpretation of Dreams* into English.

Jean-Martin Charcot (1825–93) was a French neurologist who mentored Freud. Charcot is often considered the father of neurology.

Charles Darwin (1809–82) was a British naturalist best known for outlining the principles of the theory of evolution.

Albert Einstein (1879–1955) was a German-born physicist best known for his theory of general relativity.

Sándor Ferenczi (1873–1933) was a Hungarian psychoanalyst who was one of Freud's associates in the latter stages of his life. He diverged from Freud's ideas that the psychoanalyst should be a passive participant in the process and advocated instead for a more active role.

Johann Joseph Gassner (1727–79) was an Austrian healer and exorcist. Gassner's confrontation with Franz Anton Mesmer set the stage for modern psychiatry.

Peter Gay (1923–2015) was a German American historian who specialized in European culture and intellectual history.

Queen Jocasta is a figure from Greek mythology, the wife of King Laius and mother to King Oedipus.

Ernest Jones (1879–1958) was a British psychoanalyst. Jones was also Freud's biographer.

Carl Jung (1875–1961) was a Swiss psychiatrist who was one of Freud's most prominent associates. Jung went on to establish the analytical perspective in psychiatry.

Eric Kandel (b. 1929) is an Austrian American neuropsychiatrist who won the Nobel Prize in 2000 for his research on the biological basis of memory.

King Laius is a figure from Greek mythology, the father of King Oedipus.

Karl Marx (1818–83) was a German philosopher best known for his books *The Communist Manifesto* and *Das Kapital.*

Franz Anton Mesmer (1734–1815) was a German physician who is best known for the concept of animal magnetism.

Theodor Meynert (1833–1892) was a German Austrian neuropathologist, who supervised Freud's early work in the Vienna hospital's psychiatric ward.

Anna O. was the pseudonym given to Josef Breuer's most famous patient. Her case study served as an impetus for the book he cowrote with Freud.

King Oedipus is a figure from Greek mythology. He unwittingly murdered his father, King Laius, and married his mother, Queen Jocasta.

WORKS CITED

WORKS CITED

Bassiri, Nima. "Freud and the Matter of the Brain: On the Rearrangements of Neuropsychoanalysis." *Critical Inquiry* 40, no. 1 (2013): 83–108.

Cherry, Kendra. "Books by Sigmund Freud: Freud's Most Famous and Influential Books." *About.com.* http://psychology.about.com/od/sigmundfreud/tp/books-by-sigmund-freud.htm.

"Sigmund Freud Photobiography: Freud and Jung." *About.com.* http://psychology. about.com/od/sigmundfreud/ig/Sigmund-Freud-Photobiography/Freud-and-Jung. htm.

Eidenberg, David. "Freud and Jung: A 'Psychoanalysis' in Letters." *Psychological Perspectives* 57 (2014): 7–24.

Ellenberger, Henri F. *The Discovery of the Unconscious: The History and Evolution of Dynamic Psychiatry.* New York: Basic Books, 2008.

Frank, George. "A Response to 'The Relevance of Sigmund Freud for the 21st Century." *Psychoanalytic Psychology* 25, no. 2 (2008): 375–79.

Freud, Sigmund. *The Interpretation of Dreams.* Translated by A. A. Brill. Introduction and Notes by Daniel T. O'Hara and Gina Masucci MacKenzie. New York: Barnes & Noble Books, 2005.

"Freud's book, 'The Interpretation of Dreams' released 1900." *PBS.org.* Accessed February 17, 2016. http://www.pbs.org/wgbh/aso/databank/entries/ dh00fr.html.

Freud, Sigmund, and Josef Breuer. *Studies on Hysteria.* Translated by James Strachey. London: Hogarth Press, 1955.

Gonzalez-Torres, Miguel Angel. "Psychoanalysis and Neuroscience. Friends or Enemies?" *International Forum of Psychoanalysis* 22, no. 1 (2013): 35–42.

"Historical Context for the Writings of Sigmund Freud." *Columbia College: The Core Curriculum.* http://www.college.columbia.edu/core/content/writings-sigmund-freud/context.

Jones, Ernest. "Freud and His Achievements." *The British Medical Journal* 1, no. 4974 (1956): 997–1000.

Jung, C. G. "Sigmund Freud in His Historical Setting." *Journal of Personality* 1, no. 1 (1932): 48–55.

Kandel, Eric R. "Biology and the Future of Psychoanalysis: A New Intellectual Framework for Psychiatry Revisited." *The American Journal of Psychiatry* 156, no. 4 (1999): 505–24.

Kaunders, Anthony D. "Truth, Truthfulness, and Psychoanalysis: The Reception of Freud in Wilhelmine Germany." *German History* 31, no. 1 (2013): 1–22.

Kitcher, Patricia. *Freud's Dream: A Complete Interdisciplinary Science of Mind.* Cambridge, MA: MIT Press, 1992.

Libbrecht, K., and J. Quackelbeen. "On the Early History of Male Hysteria and Psychic Trauma. Charcot's Influence on Freudian Thought." *Journal of the History of the Behavioral Sciences* 31, no. 4 (1995): 370–84.

McHugh, Paul R. "The Death of Freud and the Rebirth of Psychiatry." *TheWeeklyStandard.com*. July 17, 2000. Accessed February 22, 2016. http:// www.weeklystandard.com/article/12226.

McLeod, Saul. "Psychodynamic Approach." *SimplyPsychology*. 2007. Accessed February 22, 2016. http://www.simplypsychology.org/psychodynamic.html.

Muller, John P. "A Re-Reading of *Studies on Hysteria*: The Freud-Breuer Break Revisited." *Psychoanalytic Psychology* 9, no. 2 (1992): 129–56.

"Personality," in *Psychology*, 369–410 (Houston, TX: OpenStax College, 2014), 375.

Reppen, Joseph. "The Relevance of Sigmund Freud for the 21st Century." *Psychoanalytic Psychology* 23, no. 2 (2006): 215–16.

Ricoeur, Paul. "Sigmund Freud." In Karl Simms, *Paul Ricoeur: Routledge Critical Thinkers*, 46. Abingdon, UK: Taylor & Francis, 2002.

Solomon, Hester McFarland. "Freud and Jung: An Incomplete Encounter." *Journal of Analytical Psychology* 48, no. 5 (2003): 553–69.

Stengel, E. "Freud's Impact on Psychiatry." *The British Medical Journal* 1, no. 4974 (1956): 1000–1003.

Strenger, Carlo. "Can Psychoanalysis Reclaim the Public Sphere?" *Psychoanalytic Psychology* 32, no. 2 (2015): 239–306.

Thorne, B. Michael, and Tracy B. Henley. *Connections in the History and Systems of Psychology*. Boston, MA: Houghton Mifflin Company, 2005.

Wallerstein, Robert S. "The Relevance of Freud's Psychoanalysis in the 21st Century: Its Science and Its Research." *Psychoanalytic Psychology* 23, no. 2 (2006): 302–26.

Webster, Richard. "Freud, Charcot, and Hysteria: Lost in the Labyrinth." *RichardWebster.net*. Accessed February 22, 2016. http://www.richardwebster. net/freudandcharcot.html.

"The Well-Documented Friendship of Carl Jung and Sigmund Freud." Historacle. org. Accessed January 27, 2016. http://historacle.org/freud_jung.html.

THE MACAT LIBRARY
BY DISCIPLINE

The Macat Library By Discipline

AFRICANA STUDIES

Chinua Achebe's *An Image of Africa: Racism in Conrad's Heart of Darkness*
W. E. B. Du Bois's *The Souls of Black Folk*
Zora Neale Huston's *Characteristics of Negro Expression*
Martin Luther King Jr's *Why We Can't Wait*
Toni Morrison's *Playing in the Dark: Whiteness in the American Literary Imagination*

ANTHROPOLOGY

Arjun Appadurai's *Modernity at Large: Cultural Dimensions of Globalisation*
Philippe Ariès's *Centuries of Childhood*
Franz Boas's *Race, Language and Culture*
Kim Chan & Renée Mauborgne's *Blue Ocean Strategy*
Jared Diamond's *Guns, Germs & Steel: the Fate of Human Societies*
Jared Diamond's *Collapse: How Societies Choose to Fail or Survive*
E. E. Evans-Pritchard's *Witchcraft, Oracles and Magic Among the Azande*
James Ferguson's *The Anti-Politics Machine*
Clifford Geertz's *The Interpretation of Cultures*
David Graeber's *Debt: the First 5000 Years*
Karen Ho's *Liquidated: An Ethnography of Wall Street*
Geert Hofstede's *Culture's Consequences: Comparing Values, Behaviors, Institutes and Organizations across Nations*
Claude Lévi-Strauss's *Structural Anthropology*
Jay Macleod's *Ain't No Makin' It: Aspirations and Attainment in a Low-Income Neighborhood*
Saba Mahmood's *The Politics of Piety: The Islamic Revival and the Feminist Subjec*t
Marcel Mauss's *The Gift*

BUSINESS

Jean Lave & Etienne Wenger's *Situated Learning*
Theodore Levitt's *Marketing Myopia*
Burton G. Malkiel's *A Random Walk Down Wall Street*
Douglas McGregor's *The Human Side of Enterprise*
Michael Porter's *Competitive Strategy: Creating and Sustaining Superior Performance*
John Kotter's *Leading Change*
C. K. Prahalad & Gary Hamel's *The Core Competence of the Corporation*

CRIMINOLOGY

Michelle Alexander's *The New Jim Crow: Mass Incarceration in the Age of Colorblindness*
Michael R. Gottfredson & Travis Hirschi's *A General Theory of Crime*
Richard Herrnstein & Charles A. Murray's *The Bell Curve: Intelligence and Class Structure in American Life*
Elizabeth Loftus's *Eyewitness Testimony*
Jay Macleod's *Ain't No Makin' It: Aspirations and Attainment in a Low-Income Neighborhood*
Philip Zimbardo's *The Lucifer Effect*

ECONOMICS

Janet Abu-Lughod's *Before European Hegemony*
Ha-Joon Chang's *Kicking Away the Ladder*
David Brion Davis's *The Problem of Slavery in the Age of Revolution*
Milton Friedman's *The Role of Monetary Policy*
Milton Friedman's *Capitalism and Freedom*
David Graeber's *Debt: the First 5000 Years*
Friedrich Hayek's *The Road to Serfdom*
Karen Ho's *Liquidated: An Ethnography of Wall Street*

The Macat Library By Discipline

John Maynard Keynes's *The General Theory of Employment, Interest and Money*
Charles P. Kindleberger's *Manias, Panics and Crashes*
Robert Lucas's *Why Doesn't Capital Flow from Rich to Poor Countries?*
Burton G. Malkiel's *A Random Walk Down Wall Street*
Thomas Robert Malthus's *An Essay on the Principle of Population*
Karl Marx's *Capital*
Thomas Piketty's *Capital in the Twenty-First Century*
Amartya Sen's *Development as Freedom*
Adam Smith's *The Wealth of Nations*
Nassim Nicholas Taleb's *The Black Swan: The Impact of the Highly Improbable*
Amos Tversky's & Daniel Kahneman's *Judgment under Uncertainty: Heuristics and Biases*
Mahbub Ul Haq's *Reflections on Human Development*
Max Weber's *The Protestant Ethic and the Spirit of Capitalism*

FEMINISM AND GENDER STUDIES

Judith Butler's *Gender Trouble*
Simone De Beauvoir's *The Second Sex*
Michel Foucault's *History of Sexuality*
Betty Friedan's *The Feminine Mystique*
Saba Mahmood's *The Politics of Piety: The Islamic Revival and the Feminist Subject*
Joan Wallach Scott's *Gender and the Politics of History*
Mary Wollstonecraft's *A Vindication of the Rights of Woman*
Virginia Woolf's *A Room of One's Own*

GEOGRAPHY

The Brundtland Report's *Our Common Future*
Rachel Carson's *Silent Spring*
Charles Darwin's *On the Origin of Species*
James Ferguson's *The Anti-Politics Machine*
Jane Jacobs's *The Death and Life of Great American Cities*
James Lovelock's *Gaia: A New Look at Life on Earth*
Amartya Sen's *Development as Freedom*
Mathis Wackernagel & William Rees's *Our Ecological Footprint*

HISTORY

Janet Abu-Lughod's *Before European Hegemony*
Benedict Anderson's *Imagined Communities*
Bernard Bailyn's *The Ideological Origins of the American Revolution*
Hanna Batatu's *The Old Social Classes And The Revolutionary Movements Of Iraq*
Christopher Browning's *Ordinary Men: Reserve Police Batallion 101 and the Final Solution in Poland*
Edmund Burke's *Reflections on the Revolution in France*
William Cronon's *Nature's Metropolis: Chicago And The Great West*
Alfred W. Crosby's *The Columbian Exchange*
Hamid Dabashi's *Iran: A People Interrupted*
David Brion Davis's *The Problem of Slavery in the Age of Revolution*
Nathalie Zemon Davis's *The Return of Martin Guerre*
Jared Diamond's *Guns, Germs & Steel: the Fate of Human Societies*
Frank Dikotter's *Mao's Great Famine*
John W Dower's *War Without Mercy: Race And Power In The Pacific War*
W. E. B. Du Bois's *The Souls of Black Folk*
Richard J. Evans's *In Defence of History*
Lucien Febvre's *The Problem of Unbelief in the 16th Century*
Sheila Fitzpatrick's *Everyday Stalinism*

The Macat Library By Discipline

Eric Foner's *Reconstruction: America's Unfinished Revolution, 1863-1877*
Michel Foucault's *Discipline and Punish*
Michel Foucault's *History of Sexuality*
Francis Fukuyama's *The End of History and the Last Man*
John Lewis Gaddis's *We Now Know: Rethinking Cold War History*
Ernest Gellner's *Nations and Nationalism*
Eugene Genovese's *Roll, Jordan, Roll: The World the Slaves Made*
Carlo Ginzburg's *The Night Battles*
Daniel Goldhagen's *Hitler's Willing Executioners*
Jack Goldstone's *Revolution and Rebellion in the Early Modern World*
Antonio Gramsci's *The Prison Notebooks*
Alexander Hamilton, John Jay & James Madison's *The Federalist Papers*
Christopher Hill's *The World Turned Upside Down*
Carole Hillenbrand's *The Crusades: Islamic Perspectives*
Thomas Hobbes's *Leviathan*
Eric Hobsbawm's *The Age Of Revolution*
John A. Hobson's *Imperialism: A Study*
Albert Hourani's *History of the Arab Peoples*
Samuel P. Huntington's *The Clash of Civilizations and the Remaking of World Order*
C. L. R. James's *The Black Jacobins*
Tony Judt's *Postwar: A History of Europe Since 1945*
Ernst Kantorowicz's *The King's Two Bodies: A Study in Medieval Political Theology*
Paul Kennedy's *The Rise and Fall of the Great Powers*
Ian Kershaw's *The "Hitler Myth": Image and Reality in the Third Reich*
John Maynard Keynes's *The General Theory of Employment, Interest and Money*
Charles P. Kindleberger's *Manias, Panics and Crashes*
Martin Luther King Jr's *Why We Can't Wait*
Henry Kissinger's *World Order: Reflections on the Character of Nations and the Course of History*
Thomas Kuhn's *The Structure of Scientific Revolutions*
Georges Lefebvre's *The Coming of the French Revolution*
John Locke's *Two Treatises of Government*
Niccolò Machiavelli's *The Prince*
Thomas Robert Malthus's *An Essay on the Principle of Population*
Mahmood Mamdani's *Citizen and Subject: Contemporary Africa And The Legacy Of Late Colonialism*
Karl Marx's *Capital*
Stanley Milgram's *Obedience to Authority*
John Stuart Mill's *On Liberty*
Thomas Paine's *Common Sense*
Thomas Paine's *Rights of Man*
Geoffrey Parker's *Global Crisis: War, Climate Change and Catastrophe in the Seventeenth Century*
Jonathan Riley-Smith's *The First Crusade and the Idea of Crusading*
Jean-Jacques Rousseau's *The Social Contract*
Joan Wallach Scott's *Gender and the Politics of History*
Theda Skocpol's *States and Social Revolutions*
Adam Smith's *The Wealth of Nations*
Timothy Snyder's *Bloodlands: Europe Between Hitler and Stalin*
Sun Tzu's *The Art of War*
Keith Thomas's *Religion and the Decline of Magic*
Thucydides's *The History of the Peloponnesian War*
Frederick Jackson Turner's *The Significance of the Frontier in American History*
Odd Arne Westad's *The Global Cold War: Third World Interventions And The Making Of Our Times*

LITERATURE

Chinua Achebe's *An Image of Africa: Racism in Conrad's Heart of Darkness*
Roland Barthes's *Mythologies*
Homi K. Bhabha's *The Location of Culture*
Judith Butler's *Gender Trouble*
Simone De Beauvoir's *The Second Sex*
Ferdinand De Saussure's *Course in General Linguistics*
T. S. Eliot's *The Sacred Wood: Essays on Poetry and Criticism*
Zora Neale Huston's *Characteristics of Negro Expression*
Toni Morrison's *Playing in the Dark: Whiteness in the American Literary Imagination*
Edward Said's *Orientalism*
Gayatri Chakravorty Spivak's *Can the Subaltern Speak?*
Mary Wollstonecraft's *A Vindication of the Rights of Women*
Virginia Woolf's *A Room of One's Own*

PHILOSOPHY

Elizabeth Anscombe's *Modern Moral Philosophy*
Hannah Arendt's *The Human Condition*
Aristotle's *Metaphysics*
Aristotle's *Nicomachean Ethics*
Edmund Gettier's *Is Justified True Belief Knowledge?*
Georg Wilhelm Friedrich Hegel's *Phenomenology of Spirit*
David Hume's *Dialogues Concerning Natural Religion*
David Hume's *The Enquiry for Human Understanding*
Immanuel Kant's *Religion within the Boundaries of Mere Reason*
Immanuel Kant's *Critique of Pure Reason*
Søren Kierkegaard's *The Sickness Unto Death*
Søren Kierkegaard's *Fear and Trembling*
C. S. Lewis's *The Abolition of Man*
Alasdair MacIntyre's *After Virtue*
Marcus Aurelius's *Meditations*
Friedrich Nietzsche's *On the Genealogy of Morality*
Friedrich Nietzsche's *Beyond Good and Evil*
Plato's *Republic*
Plato's *Symposium*
Jean-Jacques Rousseau's *The Social Contract*
Gilbert Ryle's *The Concept of Mind*
Baruch Spinoza's *Ethics*
Sun Tzu's *The Art of War*
Ludwig Wittgenstein's *Philosophical Investigations*

POLITICS

Benedict Anderson's *Imagined Communities*
Aristotle's *Politics*
Bernard Bailyn's *The Ideological Origins of the American Revolution*
Edmund Burke's *Reflections on the Revolution in France*
John C. Calhoun's *A Disquisition on Government*
Ha-Joon Chang's *Kicking Away the Ladder*
Hamid Dabashi's *Iran: A People Interrupted*
Hamid Dabashi's *Theology of Discontent: The Ideological Foundation of the Islamic Revolution in Iran*
Robert Dahl's *Democracy and its Critics*
Robert Dahl's *Who Governs?*
David Brion Davis's *The Problem of Slavery in the Age of Revolution*

The Macat Library By Discipline

Alexis De Tocqueville's *Democracy in America*
James Ferguson's *The Anti-Politics Machine*
Frank Dikotter's *Mao's Great Famine*
Sheila Fitzpatrick's *Everyday Stalinism*
Eric Foner's *Reconstruction: America's Unfinished Revolution, 1863-1877*
Milton Friedman's *Capitalism and Freedom*
Francis Fukuyama's *The End of History and the Last Man*
John Lewis Gaddis's *We Now Know: Rethinking Cold War History*
Ernest Gellner's *Nations and Nationalism*
David Graeber's *Debt: the First 5000 Years*
Antonio Gramsci's *The Prison Notebooks*
Alexander Hamilton, John Jay & James Madison's *The Federalist Papers*
Friedrich Hayek's *The Road to Serfdom*
Christopher Hill's *The World Turned Upside Down*
Thomas Hobbes's *Leviathan*
John A. Hobson's *Imperialism: A Study*
Samuel P. Huntington's *The Clash of Civilizations and the Remaking of World Order*
Tony Judt's *Postwar: A History of Europe Since 1945*
David C. Kang's *China Rising: Peace, Power and Order in East Asia*
Paul Kennedy's *The Rise and Fall of Great Powers*
Robert Keohane's *After Hegemony*
Martin Luther King Jr.'s *Why We Can't Wait*
Henry Kissinger's *World Order: Reflections on the Character of Nations and the Course of History*
John Locke's *Two Treatises of Government*
Niccolò Machiavelli's *The Prince*
Thomas Robert Malthus's *An Essay on the Principle of Population*
Mahmood Mamdani's *Citizen and Subject: Contemporary Africa And The Legacy Of Late Colonialism*
Karl Marx's *Capital*
John Stuart Mill's *On Liberty*
John Stuart Mill's *Utilitarianism*
Hans Morgenthau's *Politics Among Nations*
Thomas Paine's *Common Sense*
Thomas Paine's *Rights of Man*
Thomas Piketty's *Capital in the Twenty-First Century*
Robert D. Putman's *Bowling Alone*
John Rawls's *Theory of Justice*
Jean-Jacques Rousseau's *The Social Contract*
Theda Skocpol's *States and Social Revolutions*
Adam Smith's *The Wealth of Nations*
Sun Tzu's *The Art of War*
Henry David Thoreau's *Civil Disobedience*
Thucydides's *The History of the Peloponnesian War*
Kenneth Waltz's *Theory of International Politics*
Max Weber's *Politics as a Vocation*
Odd Arne Westad's *The Global Cold War: Third World Interventions And The Making Of Our Times*

POSTCOLONIAL STUDIES

Roland Barthes's *Mythologies*
Frantz Fanon's *Black Skin, White Masks*
Homi K. Bhabha's *The Location of Culture*
Gustavo Gutiérrez's *A Theology of Liberation*
Edward Said's *Orientalism*
Gayatri Chakravorty Spivak's *Can the Subaltern Speak?*

PSYCHOLOGY

Gordon Allport's *The Nature of Prejudice*
Alan Baddeley & Graham Hitch's *Aggression: A Social Learning Analysis*
Albert Bandura's *Aggression: A Social Learning Analysis*
Leon Festinger's *A Theory of Cognitive Dissonance*
Sigmund Freud's *The Interpretation of Dreams*
Betty Friedan's *The Feminine Mystique*
Michael R. Gottfredson & Travis Hirschi's *A General Theory of Crime*
Eric Hoffer's *The True Believer: Thoughts on the Nature of Mass Movements*
William James's *Principles of Psychology*
Elizabeth Loftus's *Eyewitness Testimony*
A. H. Maslow's *A Theory of Human Motivation*
Stanley Milgram's *Obedience to Authority*
Steven Pinker's *The Better Angels of Our Nature*
Oliver Sacks's *The Man Who Mistook His Wife For a Hat*
Richard Thaler & Cass Sunstein's *Nudge: Improving Decisions About Health, Wealth and Happiness*
Amos Tversky's *Judgment under Uncertainty: Heuristics and Biases*
Philip Zimbardo's *The Lucifer Effect*

SCIENCE

Rachel Carson's *Silent Spring*
William Cronon's *Nature's Metropolis: Chicago And The Great West*
Alfred W. Crosby's *The Columbian Exchange*
Charles Darwin's *On the Origin of Species*
Richard Dawkin's *The Selfish Gene*
Thomas Kuhn's *The Structure of Scientific Revolutions*
Geoffrey Parker's *Global Crisis: War, Climate Change and Catastrophe in the Seventeenth Century*
Mathis Wackernagel & William Rees's *Our Ecological Footprint*

SOCIOLOGY

Michelle Alexander's *The New Jim Crow: Mass Incarceration in the Age of Colorblindness*
Gordon Allport's *The Nature of Prejudice*
Albert Bandura's *Aggression: A Social Learning Analysis*
Hanna Batatu's *The Old Social Classes And The Revolutionary Movements Of Iraq*
Ha-Joon Chang's *Kicking Away the Ladder*
W. E. B. Du Bois's *The Souls of Black Folk*
Émile Durkheim's *On Suicide*
Frantz Fanon's *Black Skin, White Masks*
Frantz Fanon's *The Wretched of the Earth*
Eric Foner's *Reconstruction: America's Unfinished Revolution, 1863-1877*
Eugene Genovese's *Roll, Jordan, Roll: The World the Slaves Made*
Jack Goldstone's *Revolution and Rebellion in the Early Modern World*
Antonio Gramsci's *The Prison Notebooks*
Richard Herrnstein & Charles A Murray's *The Bell Curve: Intelligence and Class Structure in American Life*
Eric Hoffer's *The True Believer: Thoughts on the Nature of Mass Movements*
Jane Jacobs's *The Death and Life of Great American Cities*
Robert Lucas's *Why Doesn't Capital Flow from Rich to Poor Countries?*
Jay Macleod's *Ain't No Makin' It: Aspirations and Attainment in a Low Income Neighborhood*
Elaine May's *Homeward Bound: American Families in the Cold War Era*
Douglas McGregor's *The Human Side of Enterprise*
C. Wright Mills's *The Sociological Imagination*

The Macat Library By Discipline

Thomas Piketty's *Capital in the Twenty-First Century*
Robert D. Putman's *Bowling Alone*
David Riesman's *The Lonely Crowd: A Study of the Changing American Character*
Edward Said's *Orientalism*
Joan Wallach Scott's *Gender and the Politics of History*
Theda Skocpol's *States and Social Revolutions*
Max Weber's *The Protestant Ethic and the Spirit of Capitalism*

THEOLOGY

Augustine's *Confessions*
Benedict's *Rule of St Benedict*
Gustavo Gutiérrez's *A Theology of Liberation*
Carole Hillenbrand's *The Crusades: Islamic Perspectives*
David Hume's *Dialogues Concerning Natural Religion*
Immanuel Kant's *Religion within the Boundaries of Mere Reason*
Ernst Kantorowicz's *The King's Two Bodies: A Study in Medieval Political Theology*
Søren Kierkegaard's *The Sickness Unto Death*
C. S. Lewis's *The Abolition of Man*
Saba Mahmood's *The Politics of Piety: The Islamic Revival and the Feminist Subjec*t
Baruch Spinoza's *Ethics*
Keith Thomas's *Religion and the Decline of Magic*

COMING SOON

Chris Argyris's *The Individual and the Organisation*
Seyla Benhabib's *The Rights of Others*
Walter Benjamin's *The Work Of Art in the Age of Mechanical Reproduction*
John Berger's *Ways of Seeing*
Pierre Bourdieu's *Outline of a Theory of Practice*
Mary Douglas's *Purity and Danger*
Roland Dworkin's *Taking Rights Seriously*
James G. March's *Exploration and Exploitation in Organisational Learning*
Ikujiro Nonaka's *A Dynamic Theory of Organizational Knowledge Creation*
Griselda Pollock's *Vision and Difference*
Amartya Sen's *Inequality Re-Examined*
Susan Sontag's *On Photography*
Yasser Tabbaa's *The Transformation of Islamic Art*
Ludwig von Mises's *Theory of Money and Credit*

Macat Pairs

Analyse historical and modern issues from opposite sides of an argument. Pairs include:

RACE AND IDENTITY

Zora Neale Hurston's
Characteristics of Negro Expression

Using material collected on anthropological expeditions to the South, Zora Neale Hurston explains how expression in African American culture in the early twentieth century departs from the art of white America. At the time, African American art was often criticized for copying white culture. For Hurston, this criticism misunderstood how art works. European tradition views art as something fixed. But Hurston describes a creative process that is alive, ever-changing, and largely improvisational. She maintains that African American art works through a process called 'mimicry'—where an imitated object or verbal pattern, for example, is reshaped and altered until it becomes something new, novel—and worthy of attention.

Frantz Fanon's
Black Skin, White Masks

Black Skin, White Masks offers a radical analysis of the psychological effects of colonization on the colonized.

Fanon witnessed the effects of colonization first hand both in his birthplace, Martinique, and again later in life when he worked as a psychiatrist in another French colony, Algeria. His text is uncompromising in form and argument. He dissects the dehumanizing effects of colonialism, arguing that it destroys the native sense of identity, forcing people to adapt to an alien set of values—including a core belief that they are inferior. This results in deep psychological trauma.

Fanon's work played a pivotal role in the civil rights movements of the 1960s.

Macat Pairs

*Analyse historical and modern issues
from opposite sides of an argument.
Pairs include:*

INTERNATIONAL RELATIONS IN THE 21ˢᵀ CENTURY

Samuel P. Huntington's
The Clash of Civilisations

In his highly influential 1996 book, Huntington offers a vision of a post-Cold War world in which conflict takes place not between competing ideologies but between cultures. The worst clash, he argues, will be between the Islamic world and the West: the West's arrogance and belief that its culture is a "gift" to the world will come into conflict with Islam's obstinacy and concern that its culture is under attack from a morally decadent "other."

Clash inspired much debate between different political schools of thought. But its greatest impact came in helping define American foreign policy in the wake of the 2001 terrorist attacks in New York and Washington.

Francis Fukuyama's
The End of History and the Last Man

Published in 1992, *The End of History and the Last Man* argues that capitalist democracy is the final destination for all societies. Fukuyama believed democracy triumphed during the Cold War because it lacks the "fundamental contradictions" inherent in communism and satisfies our yearning for freedom and equality. Democracy therefore marks the endpoint in the evolution of ideology, and so the "end of history." There will still be "events," but no fundamental change in ideology.

Macat Disciplines

Access the greatest ideas and thinkers across entire disciplines, including

MAN AND THE ENVIRONMENT

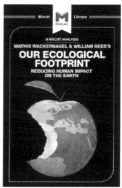

The Brundtland Report's, *Our Common Future*
Rachel Carson's, *Silent Spring*
James Lovelock's, *Gaia: A New Look at Life on Earth*
Mathis Wackernagel & William Rees's, *Our Ecological Footprint*

Macat analyses are available from all good bookshops and libraries.

Access hundreds of analyses through one, multimedia tool.
Join free for one month **library.macat.com**

Printed in the United States
by Baker & Taylor Publisher Services